# Managing Event Information

Modeling, Retrieval, and Applications

# Synthesis Lectures on Data Management

Editor
**M. Tamer Özsu**, *University of Waterloo*

Synthesis Lectures on Data Management is edited by Tamer Özsu of the University of Waterloo. The series will publish 50- to 125 page publications on topics pertaining to data management. The scope will largely follow the purview of premier information and computer science conferences, such as ACM SIGMOD, VLDB, ICDE, PODS, ICDT, and ACM KDD. Potential topics include, but not are limited to: query languages, database system architectures, transaction management, data warehousing, XML and databases, data stream systems, wide scale data distribution, multimedia data management, data mining, and related subjects.

Managing Event Information: Modeling, Retrieval, and Applications
Amarnath Gupta and Ramesh Jain
2011

Methods for Mining and Summarizing Text Conversations
Giuseppe Carenini, Gabriel Murray, and Raymond Ng
2011

Probabilistic Databases
Dan Suciu, Dan Olteanu, Christopher Ré, and Christoph Koch
2011

Peer-to-Peer Data Management
Karl Aberer
2011

Probabilistic Ranking Techniques in Relational Databases
Ihab F. Ilyas and Mohamed A. Soliman
2011

Uncertain Schema Matching
Avigdor Gal
2011

Fundamentals of Object Databases: Object-Oriented and Object-Relational Design
Suzanne W. Dietrich and Susan D. Urban
2010

Advanced Metasearch Engine Technology
Weiyi Meng and Clement T. Yu
2010

Web Page Recommendation Models: Theory and Algorithms
Sule Gündüz-Ögüdücü
2010

Multidimensional Databases and Data Warehousing
Christian S. Jensen, Torben Bach Pedersen, and Christian Thomsen
2010

Database Replication
Bettina Kemme, Ricardo Jimenez Peris, and Marta Patino-Martinez
2010

Relational and XML Data Exchange
Marcelo Arenas, Pablo Barcelo, Leonid Libkin, and Filip Murlak
2010

User-Centered Data Management
Tiziana Catarci, Alan Dix, Stephen Kimani, and Giuseppe Santucci
2010

Data Stream Management
Lukasz Golab and M. Tamer Özsu
2010

Access Control in Data Management Systems
Elena Ferrari
2010

An Introduction to Duplicate Detection
Felix Naumann and Melanie Herschel
2010

Privacy-Preserving Data Publishing: An Overview
Raymond Chi-Wing Wong and Ada Wai-Chee Fu
2010

Keyword Search in Databases
Jeffrey Xu Yu, Lu Qin, and Lijun Chang
2009

Managing Event Information: Modeling, Retrieval, and Applications
Amarnath Gupta and Ramesh Jain


ISBN: 978-3-031-00754-5    paperback
ISBN: 978-3-031-01882-4    ebook


DOI 10.1007/978-3-031-01882-4


A Publication in the Springer series
*SYNTHESIS LECTURES ON DATA MANAGEMENT*

Lecture #19
Series Editor: M. Tamer Özsu, *University of Waterloo*
Series ISSN
Synthesis Lectures on Data Management
Print 2153-5418    Electronic 2153-5426

# Managing Event Information

## Modeling, Retrieval, and Applications

Amarnath Gupta
University of California at San Diego

Ramesh Jain
University of California Irvine

*SYNTHESIS LECTURES ON DATA MANAGEMENT #19*

# ABSTRACT

With the proliferation of citizen reporting, smart mobile devices, and social media, an increasing number of people are beginning generate information about events they observe and participate in. A significant fraction of this information contain multimedia data to share the experience with their audience. A systematic information modeling and management framework is necessary to capture this widely heterogeneous, schemaless, potentially humongous information produced by many different people. This book is an attempt to examine the modeling, storage, querying, and applications of such an event management system in a holistic manner. It uses a semantic-web style graph-based view of events, and shows how this event model, together with its query facility, can be used toward emerging applications like semi-automated storytelling.

# KEYWORDS

event management system, graph data, graph query language, storytelling, event queries

*To my father,*
*who always wanted to see this day.*

*Amarnath Gupta*

# Contents

# Preface

In a loose sense, this book stems from our 20-year old work in multimedia information systems where we argued that a multimedia information system must capture not only what we perceive (like pictures and sound) but also the context in which this information exists. We argued then that most multimedia information systems of the day were focused on low-level properties of media, and they needed a more holistic information model that can capture real-world events and situations as well as objects that participate in these events because they provide the true context in which the multimedia information can be realistically interpreted and used. In the last few years, the amount of event information in the world has skyrocketed. Social media sites have pictures and videos of millions of people; mobile devices equipped with location-capturing technologies are used by billions of people to send media-rich messages about their surroundings and situations; information miners and social scientists are analyzing interesting social behavior by analyzing information from these sites and devices. Yet, interestingly, there is no formal way of "structuring" event information so that it can be effectively used for searching, querying, mining and storytelling.

This book is a result of our efforts to examine ways to develop a systematic framework in which events can be represented and analyzed, and to develop a new information management systems that is designed to model and manage information about real world events and situations that are created by thousands of ordinary situation reporters in their everyday lives. Our goal in this introductory book is to present concepts and techniques to advanced researchers as well as implementors for building event information systems. We give examples and present a first level of technical details to help in making the concepts implementable in different applications. We also discuss practical issues related to data representation, storage, and query processing. Finally, we give examples of an emerging application and actionable personal intelligence, and we show how story telling is a process of querying and synthesizing the results using event information systems that is similar to preparing reports. We hope that this book will help people interested in building event information systems. We would love to see a community of researchers and implementers who are building different applications of event information management systems. We intend to have a companion web site to share evolving knowledge as well as software and experiences in this area. We are excited about this area and hope that this excitement will be shared by many other researchers and practitioners in the community.

Amarnath Gupta and Ramesh Jain
July 2011

# Acknowledgments

We acknowledge the contributions of many our students and collaborators whose work and thoughts have been used in this book. Utz Westermann, Ansger Schrep, Arjun Satish, Setareh Rafatirad, Mingyan Gao, and Pinaki Sinha deserve special mention. Xufei Qian and Christopher Condit are software engineers who developed and implemented some of the query processing functionality described in this lecture. We have also benefited from our discussions with Prof. Michael Carey of UCI.

Amarnath would also like to acknowledge Drs. Gautam Schroff, Lipika Dey, and Hiranmay Ghosh of Tata Consulting Services Innovations Lab, New Delhi, India, for the opportunity to work with the lab on real world event management problems.

Finally, we acknowledge the patience and sacrifice of our families. We owe our deepest gratitude to Nupur, Auroni, Aurpon, Sudha, Swati, Frank, Suzi, Adolfo, and Neil, who make our lives worthwhile.


Amarnath Gupta and Ramesh Jain
July 2011

# CHAPTER 1

# Introduction

Informally, an event is something that has happened, is happening, or is expected to happen. In philosophy, an event can refer to a material phenomenon where some object changed its property, or a mental phenomenon like the occurrence of an emotion or thought. In the past decade, many different communities have defined concepts, technologies, and systems that relate to events, and they cover wide ranged areas in Computer Science including languages, databases, and communication systems [Voisard and Ziekow, 2011]. In this book, we consider events as real-world occurrences that unfold over space and time; they are observable occurrences of some phenomena that have either been explicitly recorded (e.g., "the ad hoc committee meeting occurred at 3pm on Thursday," as recorded by a person), or can be computed ("John entered room 303 through the west door" based on the computation from motion detection and face recognition routines). Typically, given a collection of events, one would want to know things like: "What happened in this event? When and where? Who was involved and how? How did it happen? What other events is this event related to and how? Who detected and reported it? What is the evidence that the event actually occurred? Does this event lead to any consequences? How do people (and machines) react to this event?" Questions like these are important in a wide variety of domains. Surveillance applications [Tian et al., 2008a] consider events like entries into and exits from a monitored space, intrusion in a prohibited regions and so on. RFID based tracking applications [Welbourne et al., 2008] consider "movement events" of objects from one place to another. Research projects on *lifelogging* such as the MyLifeBits project [Gemmell et al., 2006] from Microsoft records personal events of an individual, including the images and videos collected by the individual to capture their personal experience of events. Another class of applications, called experiential applications, focus on event-based access to live streaming multimedia information [Gupta et al., 2004]. In this case, a user might want to gain access to the live feed of a meeting when a specified event occurs. In each case, the ultimate goal of the system is to allow a user to access, search, explore, correlate, annotate, and get insight from a web of events and all their associated data.

We know about events through our senses and by hearing about event experiences of other people. With increasing use of technology, the event eco system has taken a different form than it was just a few decades ago. From the perspective of creating information systems to capture, organize, and disseminate event experiences, one can look at an *event ecosystem* as shown in Figure 1.1. Suppose that an election event takes place. For any important political event, all campaigns and speeches are captured using many photographic cameras by news agencies, TV cameras by broadcast agencies, personal cameras by spectators, and these events are broadcast using audio description among many other ways of collecting the event information. All such data go in different collections or archives

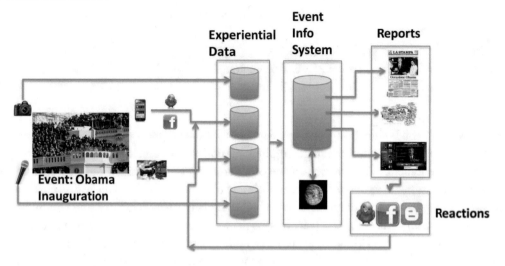

**Figure 1.1:** A cartoon schematic of an event information system. Note that there are multiple entry points to put data into such as system, and the feedbacks and event-derived information can also be placed back into the same event information system.

because videos are kept separately from articles, which are again maintained separately from public opinions coming through social media like Twitter feeds. An event information system should be created to manage all such data through a unified abstraction layer. Based on the access rights and privileges, these data are then used for preparing different reports about the event. All such reports should also become part of the information related to the event and accessible through the same information system. Despite many solutions for data federation in the commercial and academic environments, there is a lack of a principled method of modeling and designing an information system where events are first class objects. Event information systems are also equally useful for personal information. In today's world of increasing personal information acquired through multiple media devices, there is a clear need for the development of event information systems that will capture events in an individual's life, such as a wedding, to important global events that are more global but affects individual lives, like natural disasters like earthquakes and floods.

In Figure 1.2, we show a long chain of events as they connect to each other. The upper figure illustrates interconnected events around the Presidential inauguration, while the lower figure illustrates a much longer chain of events in the life of President Obama. Each important planned event usually has some pre-events as well as post-events. Though Figure 1.2 captures publicly recorded well known events, such graphs can also be constructed around the simple events in one's personal life, like having dinner and its pre and post events. In many cases, these pre and post events become as important as the event itself and need to be documented and linked to the event.

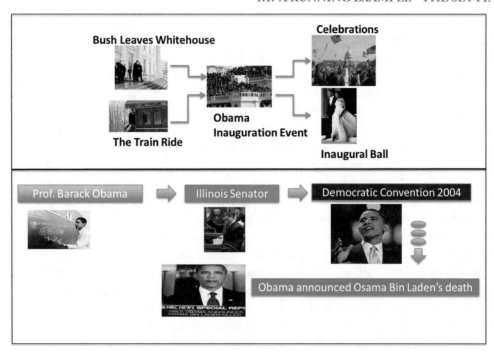

**Figure 1.2:** The top part of this figure shows a network of events related to President Obama as he takes office. The main event has several pre and post events. The bottom figure shows a potential chain of events that starts from President Obama's career as a professor to his recent announcement of the capture and death of Osama Bin Laden. Each of the events shown in the bottom figure can be 'double clicked' to expand and see many events related to that specific event, maybe resulting in structures similar to those shown in the top figure. Each events and its sub-events will be stored in the system and can be independently queried at the level of interest of a user.

A very common chain of event is linked due to *causality*. In this case, an event, say Event-1 results in Event-2, which in turn results in Event-3 and finally results in Event-N. In many applications (e.g., a dossier of a Presidential historian), it is important to discover such causal chains from the data, and analyze why a specific event occurred to a person, in politics, or in a societal debate. For these applications, it is important for an event-based system to support story analysis and event mining to determine such causal networks.

## 1.1    A RUNNING EXAMPLE – THE SETTING

Consider Newsan – an agency that collects and analyzes political information. It has an information collection team that goes to various politically important meetings, briefings, and so on and gathers information on current happenings; alongside, they capture photographs, videos and audio that they bring back to the agency. Each member of the team then creates "event records" of the information and place them into a common collection. Some of these event records are associated with pictures, audio and video recordings that have been collected by the member. Newsan also has a news watcher team that watches different broadcast channels, news web sites, political web forums, as well as web sites of politically important people and organizations. They pick potentially interesting web content, add their own annotation, describing why and what part of the content is interesting or relevant, and add them to a collection. Finally, it has an analyst team that looks through these collections and semi-automatically create "association records" among information that are related. To accomplish this, they sometimes look at past event and association records to create new association records, and sometimes they add new event records to existing association records. Some of the analysts work with customers of the agency and produce investigative event trails about specific situations, people, and groups that the customer is interested in. Very often the customers want to monitor evolving situations of interest over a considerable period of time and expect regular "summary reports" (stories) or "immediately important situation reports." Sometimes, like the analysts, the customers also expect to interactively perform interactive query/search on the system for their own analysis.

At first glance, it might seem like a standard information system design problem that can be addressed by traditional techniques. As we will show, designing event-centric systems need different modeling and design considerations. The goal of this lecture is to develop the design principles of information systems that enable this kind of applications. We will show that our event model is general enough by applying the model to different use cases, including news analysis, personal information systems, and social media. To put our model in the context of related research, we will synthesize the work of several different groups actively engaged in event-related research and develop a uniform integrated specification that captures (most of) the requirements for representing, relating, organizing, querying and reacting to event information.

## 1.2   EVENTS AND INFORMATION SYSTEMS

Information systems have been considering event management tasks for a very long time. In this section, we will present a brief tour of different sub-areas of information systems that deal with event information one way or another. These areas have evolved, sometimes independently, to cater to different information needs related to events. Therefore, their event specification methods, representations, manipulation techniques, query languages and evaluation methods are all somewhat different. In this section, we will only present a conceptual introduction to these sub-areas of information management as they relate to events, and refer back to their technical details as needed in subsequent chapters. It is important to observe the commonalities and differences between the approaches adopted by these groups and relate them to the problem of event management as we have sketched in the previous section.

## 1.2.1 ACTIVE DATABASES

Active databases, that came to light in the later part of 1980s, intended to add "behavior" to the traditional database system. While a traditional database only supported queries and updates, active databases were designed to be reactive, i.e., take an action if it encountered an event. According to the classification developed by Paton and Díaz [1999], an event can be

- a structure operation, in which case the event is raised by an operation on some piece of structure (e.g., insert a tuple, update an attribute, access a tuple),

- a behavior invocation, in which case the event is raised by the execution of some user-defined operation (e.g., the message display is sent to an object of type widget),

- a transaction, in which case the event is raised by transaction commands (e.g., abort, commit, begin-transaction),

- user-defined, in which case a programming mechanism is used that allows an application program to signal the occurrence of an event explicitly (e.g., in response to some information entered by a user),

- an exception, in which case the event is raised as a result of some exception being produced (e.g., an unauthorized access),

- clocked, or a temporal condition, which can be absolute (at a specific time), relative (5 days after a stock is sold) or periodic (every Thursday at 10 am), and

- external, in which case the event is triggered by a condition outside the database (e.g., a temperature sensor records a value greater than 37° C)

An event can also be *composite* where the composition rule is defined by an algebraic expression. In this case, the algebra involves operations like disjunction ($E_1$ OR $E_2$ occurs), conjunction ($E_1$ AND $E_2$ occurs), sequence ($E_1$ then $E_2$ occurs), closure (first occurrence of $E$ in a series of occurrences within a time window), historical aggregate (number of times $E$ has occurred within a time window), and so forth. Event algebras have been proposed by different research groups like HiPAC [Dayal et al., 1988], SAMOS [Gatziu et al., 1992], ODE [Gehani and Jagadish, 1996] and Snoop [Chakravarty et al., 1994]. In these systems, events are defined in terms of their *detection conditions*. In an active database, the typical event-related construct is that of an event-condition-action (ECA) rule of the form:

> *ON <event>*
> *CHECK <condition>* where a condition is a standard database query
> *DO <action>*, where the action can be any database operation (e.g., insert) or application operation (e.g., send email).

Notice that the main research issues in an active database system center around the details of language constructs for complex event detection, specification of the semantics of event initiation and termination conditions [Zimmer and Unland, 1999], the scheduling of rules when multiple event conditions are satisfied simultaneously, the expressiveness of the event-based rule language and that of the event composition algebra, the interaction between the rule and the event, and so forth. The focus is more on the detection and execution models of the event-based rule system and not so much on recording, classifying and inter-relating events.

## 1.2.2  COMPLEX EVENT PROCESSING

Complex event processing (CEP) is related to active database systems, but is a more general research area introduced by Luckham [2001] where an event is defined as an object that is a record of an activity in a system, and is related to other events by time, causality, and aggregation. As Rizvi [2005] points out, the focus of active database systems is on the trigger specification and processing mechanism within a DBMS; on the other hand, a CEP system considers a distributed world where events occur and notify "event handlers" who process the event and may send out their own notifications. The task of a CEP system is to still detect complex events as they occur; however, the detection will occur over multiple systems or data streams produced by streaming sources such as RSS feeds, or message streams generated by a publish-subscribe system. The inclusion of multiple sources of data leads to several new design considerations. Buchmann and Koldehofe [2009] characterize CEP as a paradigm that "decouples providers and receivers of information. Neither the providers need knowledge about the set of relevant receivers, nor do receivers need to know the set of relevant data or event sources. Second, CEP-systems do not only mediate information in form of events between providers and consumers, but support the detection of relationships among events, for instance, temporal relations that can be specified by definition of correlation rules (often called Event Patterns). Through aggregation and composition new complex events can be generated and used subsequently to derive more abstract events." IBM, for instance, has developed a CEP system, called Amit [Adi and Etzion, 2004], that defines the lifespan of a situation (i.e., a complex event) by specifying an initiation condition and a termination condition. The lifespan opened by an initiator event, however, need not represent a situation if the conditions of its termination are not met. Since the situations are defined over temporal intervals, algebraic operations over intervals (along with other event operators similar to those of Snoop [Chakravarty et al., 1994]) can be used to define a situation. Design questions for such a system center around issues like the following:

- How to support different kind of events and messages?

- How to synchronize events that arrive from different source in different time due to network delays?

- How to identify the context (temporal, semantic) in which a situation detection is relevant?

- How to change event processing rules without stopping the system (hot updates)?

- How to support vast numbers of events and conditions in an optimal way ?

- How to detect cycles in rule firing sequence?

Complex event systems have also been designed to handle streaming event data (e.g., Cayuga [Brenna et al., 2007]). In these systems, one evaluates standing queries, and the evaluation model for complex event queries is based on Nondeterministic Finite Automata (NFA) [Agrawal et al., 2008]. Oracle provides a Continuous Query Language (CQL) that enables one to match event patterns where the term "event pattern" means time sequences of values that obey certain, range, trend and duration constraints. However, none of these systems treat an event as a fundamental information unit which can be stored, queried and merged with other events. For a recent treatment of the event processing systems in the commercial world, the reader is referred to [Etzion and Niblett, 2010].

A very recent trend in CEP systems is to consider *semantic classifications and semantic associations* over events and their attributes [Teymourian and Paschke, 2009]. This research is inspired by the Semantic Web research community in building standards and tools for semantic technologies such as formalized vocabularies/ontologies and declarative rules. The goal of this approach is to develop more useful event data models by linking of the existing knowledge to any event instance. For example, an event about a stock price is connected to the semantic knowledge about the stock. This knowledge can be used for downstream event processing for tasks like event prioritization.

## 1.2.3 EVENT-ORIENTED SPATIOTEMPORAL DATABASES

A standard spatiotemporal database uses the basic model that all data objects have a (possibly complex) locational attribute and a temporal attribute that record the spatial and the valid time extent associated with the object. Many spatiotemporal information systems develop novel access methods for spatiotemporal queries. In some cases like Geographic Information Systems, the primary data object can be a spatial location which has other non-spatial and temporal properties associated with it. An event-oriented spatiotemporal database is a variant, which describes spatiotemporal data objects with "events" as a data organizing attribute. In the event-based approach introduced by Peuquet and Duan [1995] for efficiency reasons, an event is interpreted as a change in data property. ESTDM stores the time associated with each change in increasing order from the initial "world state" at time $t_0$ to the latest recorded change at time $t_n$. Worboys and Hornsby [2004] have developed an object-based event model which is designed to answer queries like the following:

- What are all the events related to object X?

- What are the objects that are related to event Y?

- Has any instance of event type Y happened without the participation of object X?

- What are all the events that are related to event Y?

More specialized data models and access methods have been developed for specific event related problems in spatiotemporal databases. Chen and Jiang [2000] analyzed the characteristics of events in land subdivision process and studied how events affect the states of spatial objects. This was used to model, store and query events and the causal relations between events and states within a spatiotemporal database system. Hornsby and Cole [2007] developed a model of event patterns that describes various kinds of object movements in an observed space. They also developed methods for composing complex event patterns from simpler patterns. Efforts like [Gutiérrez et al., 2005] and [Gutiérrez et al., 2008] develop novel indexing techniques for both standard (snapshot based) and event based queries on spatiotemporal data.

## 1.3    EVENTS AND SENSOR NETWORKS

Unlike the two previous cases where human agents provide event information to the information system, a sensor-based system deals with "raw" observations as they occur. The role of the humans is to anticipate the locations and density of sensors that will provide maximal event-bearing information for the specific problem being studied in the observed environment. A sensor network consists of a (heterogeneous) collection of spatially distributed autonomous sensors to cooperatively monitor physical or environmental conditions, such as temperature, sound, vibration, pressure, motion or pollutants. Aside from observing events for analysis, sensor based event detection may also be used for controlling the observed environment. Systems with this capability have been called *cyberphysical systems* in recent literature [Talcott, 2008].

Events can play two different roles in a sensor network based information system. In *acquisitional systems* like TinyDB [Madden et al., 2005], an event can be used to trigger data collection. For example, the query:

```
ON EVENT bird-detect(loc):
SELECT AVG(light), AVG(temp), event.loc
FROM sensors AS s
WHERE dist(s.loc, event.loc) < 10m
SAMPLE PERIOD 2 s FOR 30 s
```

can be used to report the average light and temperature level at sensors near a bird nest where a bird has just been detected. Every time a bird-detect event occurs through some external operation like a camera fitted with a motion sensing software, the query is issued from the detecting node and the average light and temperature are collected from nearby nodes once every 2 s for 30 s. Event-driven queries in TinyDB can be triggered interrupt like conditions or by polling some sensor stream. In the second case, the event itself is produced by executing a polling subquery which is periodically issued and evaluated before the acquisition query can be triggered.

In contrast, in detection systems, events are essentially query conditions that need to be evaluated over the sensor network. Events can be detected by single sensors (the temperature at a sensor location crossed a threshold value) or a collection of sensors (high average humidity from the humidity sensors in some spatial region followed by an increase in average pollutant levels from the pollutant sensors in the same region). The event detection condition in this case uses not only the values of the sensor readings but the spatial context of the sensors and the relative timing of the readings. For example, "same region" may be computed by computing the spatial overlap between the Voronoi regions determined from the locations of the humidity and the pollutant sensors. Thus, it needs to be evaluated in a distributed fashion – the query plan is broadcast to sensors through a routing tree. Each sensor host (i.e., the processor associated with the sensor) receives a query plan, determines if it is contributing to the result, and evaluates the predicates it can service, passing the result to the query host through the routing tree. This leaves a lot of room for in-network query optimization where query execution time, local storage, communication time as well as power consumption can be optimized. In the REED system [Abadi et al., 2005], developed as an extension to TinyDB, event detection algorithms take advantage of distributed join techniques, are capable of running in limited amounts of RAM, can distribute the storage burden over groups of nodes, and are tolerant to dropped packets and node failures.

A different class of event-like information is used in RFID sensor networks. Here, object locations are tracked over time and events are modeled as the states and state-transitions of these objects. Cao et al. [2009] characterize three query classes commonly found in these systems – location queries that require object location change events (e.g., "Report any pallet that has deviated from its intended path") spatial containment queries ("Verify that food containing peanuts is never exposed to other food cases for more than an hour"), and queries involves processing of sensor streams (e.g., temperature readings) in conjunction with RFID streams to detect certain event conditions ("Which pallets are exposed to environments in the warehouse where the temperature has remained more than 25 deg. over 10 hours?"). Additional complications in these systems occur because object states and transitions may contain uncertainties; hence, event pattern queries need to be evaluated with built-in uncertainty management [Agrawal et al., 2008] where events may need to be inferred using probabilistic models.

More recently, interesting applications have been developed for event monitoring in healthcare and disaster management situations. The FireStream system [Raghavan et al., 2007], for instance, designed to monitor the spread of fire, maintains three data libraries: a Spatial Store, to record structural elements and sensor locations required for spatial analysis, a Sensor Store, a collection of metadata pertinent to sensors such as thresholds and calibrations, and a Phenomenon Repository, a set of event patterns representing different classes of fire extracted from analysis of real fire datasets. These patterns represent a set of key events and event trends (i.e., time progression of events) that are used as classifiers. The actual sensor data, coming from multiple streams in a known environment, is matched against the phenomenon repository to identify the class of fire spread and use this classification for tracking the pattern of fire spread.

## 1.4 EVENTS AND MULTIMEDIA INFORMATION SYSTEMS

Researchers in Multimedia Information Systems have investigated the problem of event detection, understanding and correlation for those events that can be determined from visual and audio media (see [Xie et al., 2008] for a recent survey).

### 1.4.1   EVENTS FROM VIDEO AND AUDIO ANALYSIS

A significant body of event detection research comes from the analysis of video and audio media. The event detection and query mechanisms for these systems do not make use of any external knowledge or situation models against which events are detected and interpreted. Xie et al. [2008] identify a number of tasks are part of this class of multimedia event detection:

- model-based matching of events: extract a feature set from a multimedia resource (like a video) and then match it against a set of known event models, also represented as feature sets, to find if a certain event is occurring (e.g., is a walking event occurring?).

- event segmentation: locate a part of the data (e.g., a sequence of subregions in a sequence of video frames) where a certain event is occurring. This can be a complex task because multiple events may occur simultaneously within a single multimedia object.

- event recognition: event recognition is the process of analyzing and interpreting media content to determine the occurrence of an event as specified by a set of pre-defined models. Such an event recognition system utilizes media processing techniques like motion detection and facial recognition.

- event annotation: classify a detected event by some, potentially complex, classification criteria and then label the segmented event by its class label. Annotating events completely automatically is a research problem – practically, many event annotation systems need human input.

- event discovery: detect and recognize an event without necessarily having an a priori model of the event. The discovered event is likely to be incompletely characterized and may require human intervention.

Multimedia event detection processes are often *multi-modal*, requiring the analysis of multiple kinds of media streams, along with spatiotemporal constraints between them. A commonly researched example is in the sports domain, where a combination of object detection from visual media together with crowd reaction determination from audio leads to the detection of events like "play" in different sports [Xiong et al., 2003], or goals in soccer [Ekin et al., 2003].

   Unlike CEP or sensor network systems that work on real-world data, many multimedia systems restrict their scope to *authored media* like broadcast news and television programs, and try to detect events by exploiting the structural knowledge about the authored media. They identify events like "talking head events" in a news, "two person interview" or "conversation" that take place within a restricted setting. In the rest of this lecture, we do not consider event representations, data models or query modes for these classes of events.

### 1.4.2   EVENTS IN SURVEILLANCE SYSTEMS

Surveillance systems [Tian et al., 2008a] use many of the same principles and techniques used for regular video analysis. They are distinct from the previous class of multimedia information systems in that they explicitly use an environment model and a situation model for event detection and interpretation. An *environment model* is additional information of the space that is being monitored including all the objects that are located in the space and the zone boundaries (e.g., front door area) [Saini et al., 2009]. A *situation model* is broad class of atomic events that can be automatically detected and then variously composed to create more complex events. Therefore, tasks like event detection and tracking utilize both media-derived features, spatiotemporal correlations among features, as well as external information. This leads to a number of challenges that event-based surveillance systems have to address [Liu et al., 2009]:

- While the types of atomic surveillance events may be small, instantiating all atomic events correctly is a non-trivial problem because it depends heavily on object, object-state, and object-state-transition technologies which do not perform very well when the media data are noisy and when the density of observed objects increases. Thus, a task like watching customers for deviant activity in a crowded store is often not guaranteed to be accurate.

- In the real world, events detected from multiple cameras/sensors relating to the same object (e.g., person) must be combined to reduce uncertainty and inconsistency. For example, videos analyzed from two different subset of sensors may produce two different activity classification results if the activities have very close features. This problem gets compounded when complex events are inferred from simpler events.

- Most prototype systems developed in research labs are not designed for scalability. The efficiency and accuracy of event detection and answering events rapidly deteriorates as the number of cameras/sensors as well as the complexity of the environment model is increased.

Saini et al. [2009] have proposed a flexible architecture for event-based surveillance systems which includes a library of sensor-level atomic event detectors that populate a database of simple events per sensor type. Additionally, it has an information assimilation module so that a hierarchy of assimilated events can be computed and stored for complex event queries.

We make the observation here that event detection research usually has mostly focused on using a single kind of data (e.g., video), and the techniques applied are specific to a particular application like game analysis.

## 1.4.3  MULTIMEDIA AND SEMANTIC EVENTS

Unlike CEP systems where the need to develop techniques for semantic event characterization is recently recognized, researchers have long investigated problems related to extraction, representation and utilization of semantics of events of multimedia information [Kompatsiaris and Hobson, 2008]. The purpose behind creating semantic events in multimedia is to enable users to characterize, describe and use multimedia data in terms of human understandable terms instead of lower-level features. The expectation is that by using a standardized vocabulary of such terms (and their relationships), it will be easier for computers to exchange, interoperate and integrate multimedia information seamlessly.

A part of the effort to express and process semantic descriptions of events observed in or extracted from multimedia data is derived from MPEG-7, which is a multimedia content description standard. The standard provides a set of descriptors including semantic descriptors like places, actors, objects and events. It also has a descriptor for semantic state, which is used for the description of a state of the world described in an audiovisual segment and the parametric description of its features. A limitation of this scheme is that the definition of events is not automatically associated with time or space in which the event occurs. To address this, the DOLCE ontology [Gangemi et al., 2002] develops fundamental ontological concepts for spatial regions, temporal regions and so forth thus enabling events to be specified by referring to their spatiotemporal locale through these constructs. But even so, the specification is designed to describe the semantic content of the events within the media object and cannot relate these media-observed events to real-world events. In most of current research in multimedia semantics, the ontologies are not utilized in their full capacity. Most work concentrates on using ontologies as a vocabulary, and for lightweight inferencing.

In several small application domains (specially in sports, surveillance and news), more elaborate event structures have been developed so that segments from multiple sport videos can be interconnected by using a common semantic event ontology. In these domains, some researchers have tried to use supervised machine learning technique [Xie and Yan, 2008] for the detection of semantic objects, themes and events. However, semantic event detection schemes from general videos is still an unsolved research problem.

CHAPTER 2

# Event Data Models

As we saw in the last chapter, there is wide diversity in the way data modelers and knowledge representation researchers view events. In this chapter, we will present a number of approaches to event data modeling.

*What are we trying to model?* As we consider the different event data models, let us first consider our event modeling goals.

- Events usually involve at least one data object (including a spatial object) that is in a state for some finite amount of time (e.g., a political rally is going to occur between 2 and 4 pm today) or undergoes a change in state (e.g., a new bill was cleared by the Congress). The relationships between the objects, their states, and state changes may need to be explicitly modeled.

- Events may have a type hierarchy defined on them. For example, some event models (see later) recognize the need to show *activities* as a kind of event where some agents accomplish a task at the end of the event. Several classification systems have been developed for events. Prior research in linguistics, AI and temporal databases suggests the need to differentiate between temporal facts with goal-related semantics (i.e., *telic* such as "Bob built a house") from those that are intrinsically devoid of culmination (i.e., *atelic* such as "Bob is asleep"). Similar classifications have been made about *states* and *changes*, and *accomplishments* and *achievements*. Some of the classifications have been used in temporal databases [Terenziani et al., 2007], but a comprehensive inclusion of such classification into an event model is needed.

- Events can be connected with other events in multiple complex ways. For example, the political rally will be a protest against the bill that was passed by the Congress, but it is also a rally organized by a person who will, in the next election, stand against the senator who championed the bill. It is often important to ask "how" a set of events (e.g., the rally, the election and the clearance of the bill) are related.

- A group of inter-related events may often be grouped and collectively viewed as a bigger event. In this case, the individual members of the group are *subevents* of the grouped event. The event model needs to have provisions for event groupings.

- Inter-event relationships can have their own properties expressible through semantic rules. For example, if event $e_1$ *causes* event $e_2$, then $e_1$ must *precede* $e_2$. The event models must allow the definition of such properties and constraints. As a special case of semantic constraints, events may have properties and relationships that are dependent on time and on space and on other contextual parameters. For example, the property `leading-candidate` of an *election* event is valid only during the period for which the `election` event is valid. More correctly, it is only valid during the period when the `ballot-counting` subevent of the `election` event is valid. The event model should allow the specification of contextual properties and relationships.

- The same circumstance can be described in terms of events in many different ways, and while these are all equally valid, some may be more complex and informative than another. For example, "the candidate conceded defeat" is the same circumstance as "the candidate first challenged the election results, and then quickly retracted the challenge, and then conceded defeat in a public speech."

- Events are often witnessed through experiential information, i.e., through media like images and videos that not only make the event come alive to users, but it also allows software processes to extract event-related content from these media objects, which would otherwise be very difficult to humanly annotate. For example, the "crowdedness" of a scene is a property that is more easily computed by content processing than through human annotation. The model needs to address this event-media interaction explicitly. We will address this issue more concretely in Chapter 3.

We will start by considering a simple temporal data model because time is an essential property of events, and every event model should have a well-defined time model. Temporal data models allow querying over the changing history of data and hence consider time to be an inherent property of data elements and develop special operations to query and manipulate data elements that are dependent on time. In temporal data models, researchers consider two interpretations of time [Snodgrass and Ahn, 1986]. *Valid time* refers to the time period during which a fact is true in the real world. *Transaction time* is the time period during which a fact is stored in the database, which can be days or weeks after the fact actually occurred. A data model that captures both valid time and transaction time of its data elements is called *bitemporal*. In this chapter and throughout the book, we will only consider valid time for all data elements that have a temporal component because we are only interested in the occurrence time of events.

## 2.1    MODELING EVENTS ON TEMPORAL DATABASES

### 2.1.1    EXAMPLE: NEWSAN'S POLITICIAN DATABASE

Going back to our running example, let us assume that the Newsan agency maintains a database of party affiliations of politicians in a multi-party democracy as shown in Table 2.1 representing the relation `party-membership`. Here 'NOW' is a distinguished value that evaluates to the current date. In this table, *Name* is a non-temporal attribute, while *Party*, *Role* are temporal attributes. In this model, every tuple has a timestamp and time is represented as an interval over an absolute timeline. There can be other variations of the temporal model where attributes are timestamped [Lorentzos et al., 1995],

| ID | Name | Party | Role | From | To |
|----|------|-------|------|------|-----|
| | | | Table 2.1: Politicians and their party affiliations | | |
| 001 | N1 | P1 | Member | 03/01/1990 | 02/31/1993 |
| 001 | N1 | P2 | Member | 03/01/1993 | 06/31/2000 |
| 001 | N1 | P3 | Member | 07/01/2000 | 06/31/2002 |
| 001 | N1 | P3 | Secretary | 07/01/2002 | 04/31/2005 |
| 001 | N1 | P1 | Member | 05/01/2005 | 08/31/2005 |
| 001 | N1 | P1 | 2nd Leader | 09/01/2005 | 08/31/2009 |
| 001 | N1 | P1 | Leader | 09/01/2009 | NOW |
| 002 | N2 | P3 | Member | 02/01/1980 | 05/31/1995 |
| 002 | N2 | P3 | Secretary | 06/01/1995 | 06/31/2002 |
| 002 | N2 | P3 | Treasurer | 07/01/2002 | 04/31/2005 |
| 002 | N2 | P3 | Secretary | 05/01/2005 | 02/31/2008 |
| 002 | N2 | P3 | Leader | 03/01/2008 | NOW |

or time is represented as time instants instead of time intervals, or a nested relational model [Tansel, 1997] is used instead. While these variations lead to differences in the exact temporal operations that can be defined on the specific data model, they are not directly relevant to our current discussion. In general, most temporal databases define a set of common conceptual operations on temporal data.

1. For any event with a time interval occurrence, the begin(event) and end(event) operations, respectively, return the start and end timestamps of the event.

2. The *lifespan* of an entity is a time interval for which the entity has existed in the database. Thus, lifespan(001) = [03/1990,NOW]. Although the value of the lifespan can be computed by a coalesce operation over an ordered set of contiguous time intervals, it is a frequently used operation and merits a separate mention.

3. The *snapshot-value* of an attribute of an entity at a time instant is the value of that attribute at the specified time instance. Thus, snapshot-value(001, Party, 12/23/2001) = P3.

4. The *state-snapshot* of an entity at a time instant is a record of all attribute values of the entity at the specified time instance. Therefore, state-snapshot(001, 12/23/2001) = {Party:P3, Role:Member}. Note that in this case we did not include the attribute *Name* because it is not a temporal attribute, but there can be other interpretations where non-temporal attributes of an entity can also be incorporated as part of its state descriptor.

5. The *historical-state* of an entity is a timestamped record of all attributes values of the entity within a user-specified time interval, ordered by the start time of the record. Thus, historical-state(002, [12/23/2004,NOW]) = {(Party:P3, Role:Treasurer, [12/23/2001, 04/31/2005]),

```
(Party:P3, Role:Secretary, [05/01/2005, 02/31/2008]), (Party:P3,
Role:Leader, [03/01/2008, NOW]) }.
```

## 2.1.2    EVENTS AS VALUE CHANGES

One way to think of events based on the above data is to define them as *state occurrences* or *state transitions* that can be defined as views on this data. Inspired by the event model [Bertino et al., 1998] (although this event model is defined on an object-based data model instead of a relational one), events can be of two types: basic events and composite events. Basic events can also be of two main types: *database events* and *temporal events*. Database events can be *instantaneous* (lasting only for a time instant), reflecting an instantaneous state change and *persistent* (occurring over a period of time) reflecting a state occurrence. Temporal events can be *absolute*, *relative* or *periodic*. In our example, assuming standard date arithmetic operators, we can create an event called *party-switch*, defined as a view as follows:

```
party-switch(X,T,Pa1,Pa2) ⟵ ∃ id, role f1, t2
party-membership(id,X,Pa1,role,f1,t1) ∧ party-membership(id,X,Pa2,role,T,t2)
∧ T = t1+1, ∧ Pa1 ≠ Pa2
```

This view definition states that a *party-switch* event has occurred for a person $X$ at time $T$ if $X$ belongs to a new party $Pa_2$ the day after he belongs to the old party $Pa_1$. Similarly, one can define a view to reflect the state of the current leadership of all parties known to the database. Clearly, some events, like `party-switch` can occur multiple times in the data history. Some researchers argue that only state transitions should be considered as events. In contrast to these database events, temporal events in this event model reflect declaratively specifiable calendar and periodic expressions. For example, *8 am on the first Monday of every month* is a periodic event; *2 days after N1 became the leader of Pa1* is a relative event. Thus, a temporal event as defined in this model is a time-valued object. However, whether time-valued data objects should be considered events is a debatable event modeling issue.

Composite events, i.e., events that are defined by defining complex predicates over other atomic or complex events, are defined in Bertino-Ferari model [Bertino et al., 1998] using a number of operators.

- *Disjunction.* Event $e_1 OR e_2$ occurs if events $e_1$ or $e_2$ occurs.

- *Conjunction.* Event $e_1 AND e_2$ occurs if events $e_1$ and $e_2$ occur.

- *Sequence.* Event $e$, defined as `sequence`$(e_1, e_2, t_{min}, t_{max})$ if $begin(e_2)$ occurs within $(t_{max} - t_{min})$ of the occurrence of $end(e_1)$; as `sequence`$(e_1, e_2, t_{min}, null)$ if $begin(e_2)$ occurs at least $t_{min}$ after $end(e_1)$; as `sequence`$(e_1, e_2, null, t_{max})$ if occurs at most $t_{max}$ after $end(e_1)$; and as `sequence`$(e_1, e_2, *)$ if $begin(e_2)$ occurs any time after $end(e_1)$.

- *Occurrence.* Event `happen`$(e_1, n, e_2, e_3)$ defines $e$ to occur if $e_1$ is happening for the $n$-th time and the time interval of $e_1$ occurs within $begin(e_2)$ and $end(e_3)$. The start time for $e$ is the start time for the $n$-th occurrence of $e_1$. A special case occurs for the case $\texttt{happen}(e_1, *, e_2, e_3)$ – it means $e_1$ could have occurred any number of times.

- *Non-occurrence.* This is the negated version of the previous operation, and it is needed to ensure that a closed-world model can be applied by explicitly modeling negated events. Thus, the event $\texttt{not-happen}(e_1, n, e_2, e_3)$ starts on the ending time of $e_3$ provided $e_1$ has occurred less than $n$ times within the interval $[begin(e_2), end(e_3)]$; the event $\texttt{not-happen}(e_1, *, e_2, e_3)$ occurs if $e_1$ has not occurred within the time interval.

To illustrate these operators in our example, assume we have defined two events, *rise*(Person,Party,prev-position,new-position,Time) and *fall*(Person,Party,prev-position,new-position,Time), which detect a person changing roles in the same party, going up the command chain in the case of *rise* (e.g., from member to secretary) and getting demoted in the case of *fall* (e.g., from secretary to treasurer). We can define an event called *power-struggle* as follows:

```
power-struggle(Party,Time1,Time2) ⟵ ∃ Person1, Person2, ...
sequence(rise(Person1,Party,prev-position1,new-position1,Time1),
fall(Person2,Party,prev-position2,new-position2,Time2), null, 90)
∧ comparable(new-position1,prev-position2)
```

where the `comparable` function evaluates to true if the roles in the party are within one level of each other in the party chain of command. The event occurs if one person gains a position comparable to that held by another person within a span of 90 days after the second person gets demoted in the party.

## 2.2    MODELING EVENTS WITH CONCEPTUAL TEMPORAL MODELS

We next consider events in the context of a more complex temporal model. Such time-centric conceptual models have been developed by many research groups [Artale et al., 2007, Combi et al., 2008, Gregersen and Jensen, 1999]. Our current discussion is primarily influenced by Artale and Franconi [2009]. In the following, we assume the readers are familiar with the constructs and constraints provided by the Extended Entity Relationship model [Elmasri and Navathe, 1994]. Here we will specifically consider the *subclassOf* (i.e., IS-A) relationship, *participation constraints* (a restriction about whether all members of a class participate in a relationship), *disjointedness* (a restriction that two classes may not have common instances) and *covering constraints* (a restriction whether every instance of a class must be a member of one of its subclasses). For temporal classes (i.e., classes with temporal entities) that have timestamps, the following principles apply:

- Subclasses of temporal classes are also temporal. Therefore, if *PartyMember* is a temporal class and *partyLeader* is its subclass, then *partyLeader* is a temporal class.

- A non-temporal class may not have a temporal subclass.

- Participants of non-temporal relationships may not be temporal classes.

- If $C$ is a temporal class with subclasses $C_1, \ldots C_n$, then the subclasses can be *temporally total* (or *temporally covering*) if each member of the superclass is a member of at least one of the subclasses for at least one time instant in its lifespan [Combi et al., 2008].

- If $C$ is a temporal class with *temporally disjoint* subclasses $C_1, \ldots C_n$, then an instance $c$ of $C$ can be a member of at most one of the subclasses for all times in its lifespan [Combi et al., 2008].

- A relationship is temporal if one of the participating classes is temporal.

- A non-temporal class may have a temporal attribute. Therefore, the class *PoliticalParty* may have a temporal attribute called *RulingPeriod*.

An important class of events associated with these models are called **entity migration** or **class evolution** events, whereby an entity changes its class membership with time. Thus, a politician who moves progressively from a member subclass to a leader subclass undergoes a series of class migration events. A related class of events is **role migration**, whereby an entity changes its role in a relationship it participates in. If roles are modeled as distinct relationships, then the role migration event is equivalent to a composite event defined as *termination of participation* in one relationship followed by an *initiation of participation* in the second relationship.

One way to model these migration events is by introducing the notion of **entity status**, and status transitions. According to Spaccapietra et al. [1998], an entity status can be of four types:

1. **Scheduled.** An entity is scheduled to be in a class but the class membership will become effective only at a later time. This is the case when a party member has been elected to be a party secretary (assuming it is a temporal class), which will take effect two months after the election.

2. **Active.** The entity is the full member of the class at the current time.

3. **Suspended.** The entity is a member of the class but is currently inactive for a specified or unspecified member of the class. A cabinet member on medical leave is in a suspended status.

4. **Disabled.** The entity's membership of a class has expired and is "logically deleted." A deceased politician is disabled from a class.

For any entity instance $e$, one can group its scheduled, active and suspended status indicators for a class $C$ into an intermediate category called `exists-membership(e,C)` (which is disjoint from `disabled(e,C)`). The semantics of these status indicators are given as follows:

- Existence persists until disabled.

- Disabled persists, i.e., it will never become active any more.

- Disabled was active in the past.

- Suspended was active in the past.

- Scheduled status persists and will eventually become active.

- Scheduled can never follow active. Therefore, scheduled cannot directly evolve into a disabled status.

Migration or transition events have been modeled using the notions of **dynamic evolution** and **dynamic extension** of a class [Artale and Franconi, 2009]. Dynamic evolution occurs, as discussed before, when an object of a class $C_1$ moves to a class $C_2$ at some time $t$ and consequently leaves $C_1$ from $t + 1$. Dynamic extension occurs if an object of a class $C_1$ now becomes a member of class $C_2$ at some time $t$, but it still retains its membership of $C_1$ beyond time $t$.

A different category of events can be defined in terms of processes represented by a class of relationships called **generative relationships**. These temporal relationships are instantaneous in time and lead to the creation of new entities from existing entities. The splitting of a political party is an example where the relationship between the original party and the new party is generative. Clearly, the target class (i.e., the class to which an object belongs after the relationship takes effect) cannot be disabled. Generative relationships can be further specialized into **production** and **transformation** relationships. The former refers to the creation of a new entity while the latter refers to an existing entity becoming a new entity. For example, the relationship {GovernmentAgency *commissions Investigation*} is a production relationship because it creates a new investigation entity. On the other hand, {GovernmentAgency *reorganizes-into* GovernmentAgency} is a transformation relationship. From our standpoint, every instantiation of these relationships can be viewed as a state change or an event.

## 2.3    E* – A GRAPH-BASED EVENT MODEL USING RDF AND ONTOLOGIES

In the previous models, events were viewed as changes in a value (relational model) and transitions of class memberships, or participation in relationships. A different perspective of modeling comes from the observation that in many real-life systems, the number of relationships involved is quite large and cannot be completely estimated at design time. This requires a data model where relationships between objects need to be explicitly modeled and the properties of relationships can be logically described as part of the model. For example, one can explicitly declare a relationship to be transitive, a functionality that cannot be captured directly in a relational model. A number of groups have addressed this problem by adopting an graph based data model of objects (i.e., entities), object-states and events. Many of them (e.g., [Perry, 2008, Scherp et al., 2009a, van Hage et al., 2011]) use RDF (Resource Description Format), a World Wide Web standard for the Semantic Web, as the primary formal structure for representing and querying over graphs to satisfy the above requirements. Graph based representations are suitable for cases where the number of relationships between data

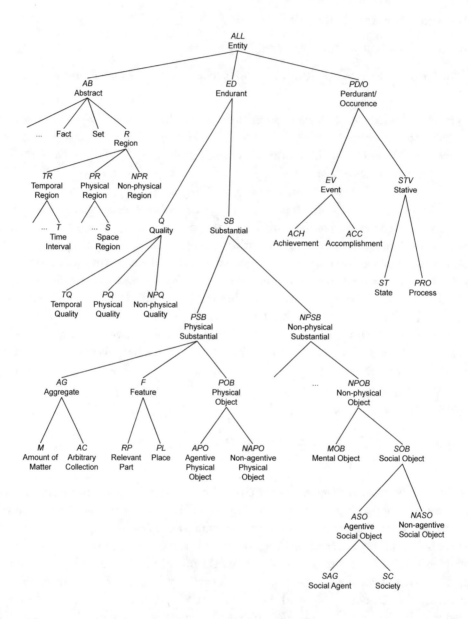

**Figure 2.1:** A portion of the DOLCE upper ontology used in the E* event data model from [Gangemi et al., 2002]. The edges denote the *subclass* relationship.

objects is very large, graph-traversal is important for query evaluation, and graph properties can be used to query, infer and analyze data. In addition, many of these groups consider a knowledge model for describing and querying events and adopt the Web Ontology Language (OWL) as the formal knowledge representation model which is also graph structured, and lends itself to a limited form of logical inferencing.

We present a graph-based, semantic event data model called E*, an extension of the E event model [Westermann and Jain, 2007]. Since our model is graph based, users can define any number of relationships between entities as needed by the applications. Since the model is semantic, i.e., based on an ontology, all system-defined relationships have formally-defined properties, and any application-defined property can also be described formally. Our ontological extensions of the E event model are partly drawn from the work of [Wang et al., 2005a,b] which itself is based on the ABC ontology [Lagoze and Hunter, 2001]. We also draw from basic concepts in the DOLCE upper ontology [Gangemi et al., 2002] and the work of Perry [2008] that develops an RDF-based data model to represent spatial, temporal and thematic relationships between data objects. There are related efforts by Salguero et al. [2009] and Batsakis and Petrakis [2010] who extend the OWL ontology language to present spatiotemporal relationships and their properties. A major difference between this ontological model with the previous spatiotemporal data models is that states, events and elements of the event are directly represented as first class model constructs and not inferred entities derived from changes in value or class membership. The E* model is graph-based so that it can model inter-event relationships flexibly, and it is ontological so that the logical constraints imposed by inter-entity relationships can be captured by the conceptual model, and be used by the application that would be built on the event model.

In DOLCE [Gangemi et al., 2002], the universe consists of entities that are further categorized into **endurants** which are objects that persist in time, **perdurants** (also called **occurrents**), which are happenings that live only within specified time intervals, and **abstract** that are entities corresponding to regions (e.g., a temporal region, a spatial region). Unlike perdurants, if two endurants occupy exactly the same space at the same time, they must be the same object. An endurant in DOLCE can be either a *substantial* (e.g., a physical object) or a *quality*, where the term quality refers to entities we perceive or measure like shape, color, mass, length, and so forth.

*In E*, an event is a perdurant, i.e., a temporal entity.*
Perdurants are characterized in DOLCE by two properties called *homeomericity* and *cumulativity* [Masolo et al., 2003]. A perdurant is *homeomeric* if and only if all its temporal parts are described by the very expression used for the whole perdurant. Every temporal portion of the perdurant "An investigation is going on against politician P1" is still described by "An investigation is going on against politician P1." If the (mereological[1]) sum of any two perdurants of type $\tau$ is a perdurant of type $\tau$ then all perdurants of type $\tau$ are **stative (or cumulative)**; otherwise they are **eventive**. Thus, a perdurant of type "standing" is stative, but that of type "speaking" is not because two consecutive time intervals within a "speaking" event may have a non-speaking event like a pause. If all (mereological)

---

[1]Mereology is the study of parts and wholes.

parts of a stative perdurant of type $\tau$ are of type $\tau$, then the perdurant is a **state**; otherwise, the perdurant is a **process**. Thus, "being the Party leader" depicts a state while "traveling from Amsterdam to New York" is a process (because the initial and the final states of the traveler are different). If an eventive perdurant has no proper parts, then it is called an **achievement**; otherwise, it is an **accomplishment**. Meetings, ascents, and performances are examples of accomplishments. Acts of reaching (e.g., a reaching a multi-party consensus), retirements, and deaths are examples of achievements. To be consistent with this terminology, *an event in the E\* model is an eventive perdurant.*

Since E\* is roughly based on an RDF-style graph-structured model, we provide a brief introduction to RDF in Appendix A. We point out that the E\* graph model does not admit a reflexive relationship.

### 2.3.1  EXAMPLE: NEWSAN COVERS A RALLY THAT TURNED VIOLENT.

An agent of Newsan went to TroubleTown, 60 miles east of StateCapital on September 12, 2010 to cover a rally by EthnicMinority, a group that called the rally to protest against the noReservation law passed by the Government three days back. The rally started at 2 pm. The main speaker EthnicLeader made some inciting comments about how the Government must be stopped from doing its regular business unless the job reservation demands of the group were met. Twenty minutes into the speech, a section of the crowd grew violent and started throwing stones at city buses. Soon the violence spread, and within the next half hour, the mob set fire to a police vehicle, damaged a fire truck and some private vehicles. The police immediately started firing in the air to disperse the crowd and called for additional forces. The violence was brought under control an hour after the additional forces arrived. Later, EthnicMinority reported that several rally-goers were injured from the clash with the police. At a press conference at 6 pm, EthnicLeader denounced the Government's "unlawful use of force" on minorities.

Table 2.2 shows the different modeling categories we described earlier and their data instances as found in the example.

To get a proper understanding of these categories, their semantics and inter-relationships in our context, we first need to develop the models for time and location, which are essential components (called *facets*) of an event model [Westermann and Jain, 2007].

### 2.3.2  MODELING TIME IN E\*

E\* uses a time interval model for absolute time, which is represented by the standard attribute-pair start-time, end-time. If either of the values are missing, it is represented by the constant T_UNK if the value exists but is not known, or by the constant T_NSP, if the value cannot be specified. Further, the model also allows for *named time intervals* and *relative time intervals*. A named time interval is an association between a named enity (e.g., "Independence Day," "winter recess of the Parliament") and a time interval. The value of the time interval for the named entity may be determined statically (as in the case of "Independence Day" of a specific country), or it may be determined dynamically by computing from other data (as in the case of "winter recess of the Parliament"). A relative time

Table 2.2: Data Objects and their model categories

| Model Category | Data Elements | Comment |
|---|---|---|
| endurant | EthnicMinority, police, crowd, car, bus, fire truck, private vehicles ... | later we will deal with the fact that police, crowd and private vehicles are anonymous groups |
| state | speech, end of violence | |
| process | violence-spread | the spread of anything is a process because its terminal state is different from its initial state |
| event | rally, stone pelting, police firing, clash with police... | each of these events has subevents |
| achievement | injury, violence control | these are achievements because they have no proper subpart |
| accomplishment | police actions, stone pelting | police actions are composed of multiple types of temporal subparts |

interval is a time interval that is associated with a reference time interval through a function. Thus, "three days after the law passed" is a relative time that can be resolved if the date/time of the passing of the law is known to the system; otherwise, it is maintained as a relative fact. Since in all cases, time refers to calendar date-time, a reference time zone may be optionally specified for time disambiguation.

A *temporal statement* is a simple temporal RDF statement as shown in Figure 2.2. In this example, both an absolute time and a relative time are recorded for the event `rally` because they carry different information content. Notice the temporal reification (a standard transformation where a new temporal entity will be created and associated with a number of existing entities) where the intervals of occurrence are given their own identifiers. The property *occurs_during* maps a perdurant to the time interval of its occurrence. The association between perdurants and time intervals can be modeled in multiple ways. Perry [2008] uses the RDF reification mechanism by which one declares an RDF sentence (the reified object) and associates an RDF triple with it. A second way is to use extensions of RDF (e.g., Annotated RDF [Udrea et al., 2010] that generalizes the model of temporal RDF [Gutierrez et al., 2007]) where the edge of an RDF graph can be associated with additional properties. We show a more complex example of temporal information modeling in Figure 2.3 where we use the RDF reification method to model the information in the statement "EthnicMinority reported that several rally-goers were injured from the clash with the police."

In this example, the label *patient* depicts a relationship from an agent of an action (in this case, the injury) to the receiver on who the action was inflicted (in this case, the injured people). Let us consider *occurs_during* and *subevent-of*, two fundamental relationships associated with events.

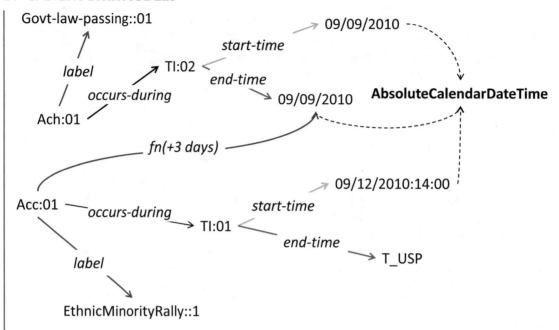

**Figure 2.2:** The structure of a simple temporal statement in the E* model. Acc, Ach stand for accomplishment and achievement respectively. The construct $fn(\phi)$ where $\phi$ is a temporal expression, indicates relative time. The "language" to represent relative time consists of standard temporal predicates like before, after, often in conjunction with arithmetic expressions.

If $P$ is a perdurant and $I$ is a time interval, then $occurs\_during(P, I)$ has the following semantics:

$$\forall t \sqsubset_T I, occurs\_during(P, I) \implies occurs\_during(P, t)$$

where $\sqsubset_T$ is a temporal subinterval relationship. Thus, $occur\text{-}during$ implies a universal quantification over time intervals. If we wanted to say that $P$ occurs sometime within the duration of $I$, the existential quantification is written as $occurs\_sometime\_during(P, I)$. A numerically quantified version of the $occurs\_during(P, I)$ predicate is written as $occurs\_during\_n(P, I, n)$ with the additional constraint $\phi(n)$ where $\phi(n)$ is an arithmetic formula like $(n \geq 3)$. This means that $P$ occurs at least 3 times during the specified time interval.

The relationship *subevent-of* (more on subevents in Section 2.3.4) is an irreflexive, asymmetric and transitive relationship between a pair of events. The acyclicity of the relationship can be fruitfully exploited during query processing, as we will see in the next chapter. Thus, $subevent\text{-}of(E_1, E_2) \wedge subevent\text{-}of(E_2, E_3) \implies subevent\text{-}of(E_1, E_3)$. Further, the *subevent-of* relationship has the following entailment rule:

$$\frac{event(A), event(B), subevent - of(B, A)}{(B.start\_time \geq A.start\_time) \wedge (B.end\_time \leq A.end\_time)} \tag{2.1}$$

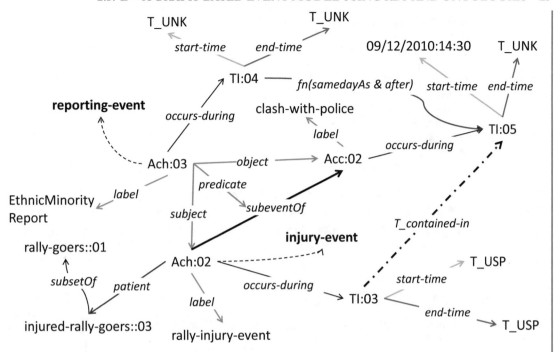

**Figure 2.3:** The structure of a reified temporal statement in the E* model. The bold edge designates the actual "claim" of the report that the injury event was a subevent of the clash event. Here the bold-lettered terms are assumed to be part of the *domain ontology* that is logically connected to the DOLCE upper level ontology.

Therefore, the temporal interval of the injury event is contained in the temporal interval of the clash. This is shown with a bold dashed edge between the corresponding time-interval objects. The temporal constraint states that while the exact time of the reporting is not known, it is on the same day and after the occurrence of the clash event (`samedayAs` and `after` are both built-in temporal expressions in E*). Not shown in the figure is the assertion that `rally-goers` is an application-level dynamic entity because `rally-goers` is a collection of enity type `rally-goer` which, in turn, is a *temporal role* played by a `person` entity in some interval(s) of time. Although these examples apply to events, stative perdurants (DOLCE ontology [Gangemi et al., 2002]) are modeled in the same way. To see how stative perdurants are represented in the E* model, consider the tuple

    politician-db(001, N1, P3, Member, 07/01/2000, 06/31/2002)

from Newsan's politician database. Using the N-triple syntax of RDF, the complete information contained in the tuple will be represented in E*:

    (soc-agent:001 instance-of politician)
    (soc-agent:001 has-name N1)

```
(soc-agent:005 instance-of political-party)
(soc-agent:005 has-name P3)
(soc-agent:001 has-state S1)
(S1 instance-of stative-sentence)
(S1 occurs_during TI1)
(TI1 start-date 07/01/2000)
(TI1 end-date 06/31/2002))
(soc-agent:001 member-of soc-agent:005)
(S1 subject soc-agent:001)
(S1 predicate member-of)
(S1 object soc-agent:005)
```

Note in this example how the state is encoded as a ***stative sentence***, a subproperty of an rdf:sentence that has a temporal duration as well as an incident property called *has-state*. E* adopts the modeling pattern of specializing the rdf:sentence to model spatiotemporal and perdurant properties. Since the perdurant is explicitly modeled as stative, it is constrained by definition not to have any further subevents.

### 2.3.3    MODELING LOCATION IN E*

Location is modeled similarly as time. E* adopts and extends Perry's model [Perry, 2008] of spatial entities, which is derived from GeoRSS GML ontology, and is represented in Figure 2.4.

Note in this figure that located-at is a spatial relationship, modeled using the RDF N-triple format as follows:

```
(NamedPlace located-at SpatialRegion)
(TS1 rdf:type temporalSentence)
(TS1 subject NamedPlace)
(TS1 predicate located-at)
(TS1 object SpatialRegion)
(TS1 occurs_during TR1)
(TR1 start-time ts)
(TR1 end-time te)
```

where a ***temporal sentence*** is an E* property defined as a subproperty of rdf:sentence (see Appendix A) that has a mandatory property occurs_during which connects it to a time interval. An analogous and commonly used relationship between two named places is located-in. By definition, if $A$, $B$ are named places then

$$(A \text{ located-in } B) \quad \Longrightarrow \quad \exists sr_1, sr_2, T_1, T_2 \ (A \text{ located-at} [T_1, T_2] \ sr_1) \ \wedge$$
$$(B \text{ located-at} [T_1, T_2] \ sr_2) \ \wedge \ \text{S\_contained\_in}(sr_1, sr_2)$$

where S_contained_in designates spatial containment.

In addition to a coordinate system, sometimes a spatial region will be parcellated into a set of polygonal regions, and the location of an entity is identified by the parcel where it occurs. For example, the police beat of a city is parcellation, which again is distinct from the voting district parcellation of the same region. In many cases, the latitude-longitude style point position is not appropriate for describing an event, and the atomicity of the spatial descriptor is maintained at the

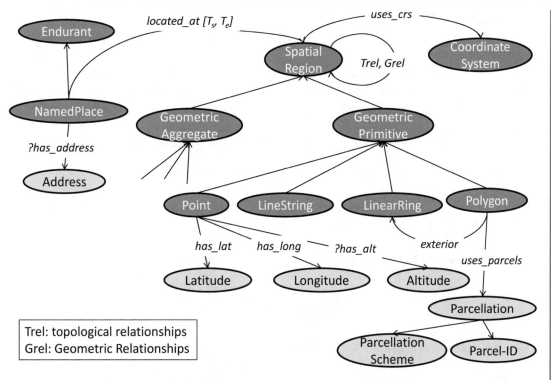

**Figure 2.4:** The Space Model from E*, adapted from [Perry, 2008]. The entity classes represented in darker ellipses belong to the upper ontology of E*. The property names starting with a ? are considered optional. Not shown in the figure are three subtypes of geometric-aggregates, multi-point, multi-lineString and multi-polygon.

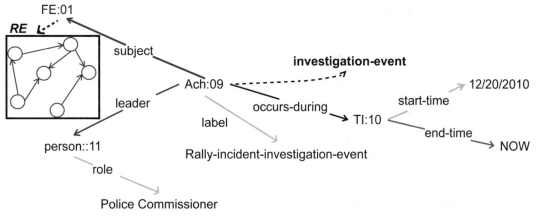

**Figure 2.5:** Ach:10 is the investigated led by the police commissioner after the rally violence. The graph called RE represents Figure 2.3 and is folded into the node FE:01.

level of the parcels. This is captured in 2.4 through the *uses-parcellation*($R$, $S$, $id$) relationship where $R$ is region of interest, $S$ is the parcellation scheme (e.g., police beat) used and $id$ is the parcel identifier within scheme $S$.

Just as *occurs_during* is an association between a perdurant and a time interval, the relationship *occurs_at*($P$, $R$) is a relationship that maps a perdurant $P$ to a named location or a spatial region designated as $R$. The properties of the *occurs_at* relationship is similar to *occurs_during*:

- *occurs_at*($P$, $R$) means $P$ occurs at any subspace $r$ of $R$ (designated as $r \sqsubseteq_S R$).

- *occurs_somewhere_at*($P$, $R$) means $P$ occurs somewhere within $R$.

- *occurs_at-n*($P$, $R$, $n$) together with an arithmetic constraint $\psi(n)$ means $P$ occurs $n$ places within $R$ obeying the constraint $\psi$.

- It interacts with the *subevent-of* relationship similarly as rule 2.1:

$$\frac{event(A),\ event(B),\ subevent - of(B, A)}{S\_contained\_in(B.located - at,\ A.located - at)} \tag{2.2}$$

These examples also illustrate the relationship families TRel (topological relationships like *S_contained_in* in the violent rally example) and Grel (geometric relationships) (e.g., "60 miles east of" in the same example). These relationships, together with arithmetic expressions, express relative locational relationships, and are often computed on the fly rather than asserted in the database, but for our purposes, we treat them as any other RDF property. A relative spatial location can also be specified by user-defined spatial properties without using topological and geometric relationships. To state that event event:01 occurred inside the kitchen of the second wing of third floor of the building named "Kennedy House," we can use the RDF description:

```
(phys-obj:01 instance-of building)
(phys-obj:01 has-name ''Kennedy House'')
(phys-obj:01 located-at sp-reg:01)
(reg:02 located-in phys-obj:01)
(reg:02 instance-of building-floor)
(reg:02 has-floor-number 3)
(reg:03 instance-of kitchen)
(reg:03 located-in reg:02)
(reg:03 has-wing-number 2)
(event:01 occurs_at reg:03)
```

where has-floor-number, has-wing-number are application-specific location-describing properties. But since their types are known from a domain model (e.g., it is known that "kitchen" is a spatial region inside a building) the overall description is logically consistent, and we can infer that the event took place at the same latitude and longitude as the building (approximately).

## 2.3.4   MODELING GRANULARITY OF PERDURANTS

We use the term **granularity** to refer to the level of detail in which entities and their relationships are described in an information system. As a simple example, one can refer to the clash between the police and the rally goers as a single event; alternatively, one can consider "smaller" events like "a section of the crowd getting violent," "part of the crowd throwing stones," "burning of private vehicles," and choose to model them as eventive information entities that relate to each other. In this case, the latter model will be considered more granular than the clash event. The framework for granularity modeling is partly derived from the formal theory of granularity proposed by Keet [2008], much of which is based upon the DOLCE ontology.

Clearly, not all perdurants can be granularized. An atomic state, or an achievement, cannot have finer granularity, unless their class memberships are updated. We call all non-atomic perdurants as *granularizable*. The granulation of these perdurants can be performed in at least three different ways.

- **Granulation through subevents.** The *subevent-of* relationship $\preceq_E$ is essentially a parthood relationship forming a directed acyclic graph such that $e_1 \preceq_E e_2$ means $e_2$ has a finer level of granularity than $e_1$. However, by itself the $\preceq_E$ relationship is not scale-dependent, i.e., $e_1 \preceq_E e_2$ does not imply that $e_2$ occurs at a finer spatial or temporal scale than $e_1$. From rule (2.1), if $e_2, e_3 \preceq_E e_1$ then either the time intervals corresponding to $e_2, e_3$ overlap, or one of them follows the other. We have presented several examples of *subevent-of* relationship in this section. Later in this section, we will provide a more complete characterization of this relationship.

- **Granulation through aggregation.** Granulation occurs through aggregation when a larger eventive perdurant can be viewed as a *collection* of smaller eventive perdurants. For example, the eventive perdurant "political protests in the state" is a collection of "political protest" events in the counties, which is a collection of similar events in the cities and so forth. These protest events are potentially unconnected and hence cannot be viewed as subevents of the larger event. Thus, this granulation mechanism represents an irreflexive, non-symmetric, transitive relationship called *subcollection-of*, designated by the symbol $\subset_C$.

- **Granulation through folding.** A more general form of granulation is *folding* which is a graph contraction operation where a subgraph of an event graph is contracted into a single event node using user-defined *folding functions*. For example, consider the event graph in Figure 2.5 showing an investigation event that occurred after violence broke out in the rally we described before. The event referred to as FE:01 is the folding of the event graph shown in Figure 2.3. The folding function in this case may be represented by a query that assigns the 3-neighborhood subgraph of the event Ach:03 in Figure 2.3 to the folded node FE:01. In [Wang et al., 2005a], the grouping of a chain of finer perdurants into a higher-level, folded perdurant is called a *track*. In our model, we represent folding as a hierarchical graph, where the hierarchy defining relationship is called *folded-into*, designated as $\prec_f$.

To completely characterize the properties of these granularity mechanisms, we must investigate the relationship between these mechanisms and the partitionability of the spatial and temporal regions, and parthood properties of agentive endurants that participate in granularizable perdurants.

**Granulation of Time.** The granulation of time has been studied by a number of research groups [Bettini et al., 1997, Combi et al., 2004, Merlo et al., 2000, Pfennigschmidt and Voisard, 2009]. All models exploit the fact that time is an ordered, hierarchically partitionable domain, and any granularity function must have a way of covering the time axis. It is customary for many database and data warehousing to offer a standard granularity scheme with *month-day-hour-minute-second* as granularity levels, where each level satisfies the definition of granularity stated below.

Informally, a granule is an atomic quantum of time (also called a *chronon* such that any two time points smaller than the quantum are considered indistinguishable). Formally, a ***temporal granule*** is a non-empty subset of the time domain, and granularity is commonly defined to be a mapping $G$ from integers, called the *index set*, to subsets of the time domain, such that: (1) if $i < j$ and $G(i)$ and $G(j)$ are not empty, then each element of $G(i)$ is less than all elements of $G(j)$, and (2) if $i < k < j$ and $G(i)$ and $G(j)$ are not empty, then $G(k)$ is not-empty. The following relationships are defined for temporal granularity [Pfennigschmidt and Voisard, 2009]:

1. *Subgranularity.* A granularity level $G$ is called a subgranularity of a granularity level $H$, denoted $G \sqsubset_T H$, if the set of granules of $G$ is a subset of the set of granules of $H$.

2. *Finer than.* A granularity $G$ is called finer than a granularity $H$, denoted $G \preceq_T H$, if for every granule $G(i)$ of $G$ there exists a granule $H(j)$ in $H$ such that $G(i)$ represents a subset of $H(j)$. $\preceq_T$ is an reflexive, asymmetric, transitive relationship.

3. *Groups into.* A granularity level $G$ is said to group into a granularity level $H$, written $G \lhd H$, if all granules of $H$ can be represented by the union of a set of granules of $G$. Thus, days group into months, days also group into weeks. The hierarchy induced by recursive grouping of granularity levels is called the *granularity hierarchy*.

4. *Partitions.* A granularity $G$ partitions a granularity $H$ if $G \lhd H$ and $G \preceq H$. In this case, both granularities cover exactly the same portion of the time domain image[2], i. e., the images of $G$ and $H$ are identical.

5. *Covered By.* A granularity $G$ is covered by a granularity $H$ if the image of $G$ is a subset of the image of $H$.

One can define a *coarsen(data, fromLevel, toLevel)* operation that changes the granularity of a temporal value from a lower level to a higher (coarser) level in the granularity hierarchy (e.g., see [Pfennigschmidt and Voisard, 2009] for one such algorithm). We will use the above relationships and operation to relate events that are described at different granularity levels. For simplicity, we will avoid cases where granularities allow gaps and overlaps among granules at the same level [Combi et al., 2004, Merlo et al., 2000].

---

[2]The term time domain image refers to the extent of time for which both $G$ and $H$ are defined.

**Granulation of Spatial Regions.** Granulation of spatial regions is more complex because space is a multidimensional entity that is not ordered, and varying the resolution of observation impacts which objects within the spatial region can be observed, and how these objects should be represented. For instance, what appears to be a point at one resolution may appear to be a polygon at a fine resolution and a multipolygon at an even finer resolution, thus making the granularity and granule description dependent on the scale at which the region is observed.

Camossi et al. [2006] defines spatial granularity as follows. Let $\mathcal{IS}$ be an index set, e.g., the set of natural numbers $\mathbb{N}$. Let the spatial domain be homeomorphic to $\mathbb{R}^2$. A **spatial granularity** $G_s$ is a mapping $\mathcal{IS} \rightarrow 2^{\mathbb{R} \times \mathbb{R}}$, the powerset of the spatial domain, and the following condition holds:

if $i < j$, and $G_s(i)$ and $G_s(j)$ are non-empty granules of granularity $G_s$, then $G_s(i)$ and $G_s(j)$ are disjoint, i.e., $(G_s(i) \cap G_s(j) = \emptyset)$.

The above condition states that two spatial entities of the same granularity cannot overlap. As before we can define the spatial version of a *finer than* relationship $G \preceq_s H$ between a pair of granularity levels. As in the case of $\preceq_T$, $\preceq_s$ is anti-reflexive and transitive, and thus induces a lattice over a collection of granularities.

An important consideration for spatial granularities is the impact of "zooming in" or "zooming out" – resulting in the change in granularity of observed spatial entities. Since spatial entries involve geometries, the effect of "zooming" can change the geometric character of the entity due to the change in scale. Camossi et al. [2006] captures this in the form of **granularity conversion operations**. Some of their conversion operators (duly adapted to suit our purposes) are given below:

- *thinning*($l, g_{fine}, p, g_{coarse}$): a linear region $l$ at granularity $g_{fine}$ is thinned to a point $p$ at a coarser granularity $g_{coarse}$. The inverse function is *expand*($p, g_{coarse}, l, g_{fine}$).

- *thinning*($r, g_{fine}, p, g_{coarse}$): a polygonal region $r$, together with its boundary $c$ at granularity $g_{fine}$ is thinned to a point $p$ at a coarser granularity $g_{coarse}$. The inverse function is *expand*($p, g_{coarse}, l, g_{fine}$).

- *merge*($l_1, l_2, \delta, g_{fine}, l_m, g_{coarse}$): two linear regions within a linear distance of $\delta$ from each other at granularity $g_{fine}$ are merged into a single linear region $l_m$ at a coarser granularity $g_{coarse}$. The inverse function is *split*($l_m, g_{coarse}, l_1, l_2, g_{fine}$).

- *merge*($r_1, r_2, g_{fine}, r_m, \delta, g_{coarse}$): two polygonal regions within a distance of $\delta$ from each other at granularity $g_{fine}$ are merged into a single region $r_m$ at a coarser granularity $g_{coarse}$. The inverse function is *split*($r_m, g_{coarse}, r_1, r_2, g_{fine}$).

- *eliminate*($p, g_{fine}, g_{coarse}$): a point $p$ visible in granularity $g_{fine}$ becomes eliminated at a coarser granularity $g_{coarse}$. The inverse function is *insert*($p, g_{fine}$).

To illustrate these operations in the context of events, consider that 10 public protests have broken out in different parts of a city $C$ on the same day. A *thinning* operation can collapse these events to a coarser granularity, where the city $C$ is considered to be an indivisible point object where all 5 events take place. This operation will lose the spatial details of where the events occurred within the city. The *merge* operation achieves coarsening somewhat differently. Consider the same 10 protests but consider their spatial extents are specified by city blocks. If $\delta$ is set to 3 miles, then city blocks less than three miles apart from each other are fused by the *merge* operation, and the event count for this new subdivision of the city is recomputed. After the fusion, each event will be associated with a larger spatial extent than one city block. The *eliminate* operation can be used to produce the "zoom out" effect discussed earlier. Consider an event like the occurrence of brush fire over a district. If we set the minimum granularity of the fire burning events to a 5 mile radius, then a small local fire damaging a hundred square yards can be eliminated from the event list because it is too small to count within the specified granularity.

**Semantic Granularity of Endurants.** Endurants are an inevitable part of events because they participate in events and become part of events in many different ways. In order to fully define the role of endurants in events, we must consider that endurants can also be viewed as entities that can be described in different granularities. Here we consider the two most common axes of endurant granularity.

Endurants, irrespective of their subtypes, are either collections or individuals. For collections, one way to describe granularity is to divide them into subcollections based on some criteria. In the example of the violent rally, the subgroup of rally-goers that started throwing stones is one such sub-collection. The *subset-of*$(X, Y, \phi)$, where $X, Y$ are collections and $\phi$ is a predicate representing the subset selection criteria. From an RDF viewpoint, this can be expressed as a triple (X, *subset-of:$\phi$* Y), where $\phi$ acts as an addition to the edge-label *subset-of*. In Figure 2.3, $\phi$ is not specified due to lack of space, but it is defined by the condition $X \leftarrow Y \cap isInjured()$, so that only injured people of $Y$ is included in $X$. Since standard RDF does not allow the inclusion of additional structure that annotates the edge label, we use the formalism called Annotated RDF [Udrea et al., 2010] (or aRDF). In essence, an aRDF triple consists of an ordinary RDF triple together with an annotation (member of an annotation class $\mathcal{A}$). In the context of aRDF, annotations can be thought of as a partially ordered set $(\mathcal{A}, \preceq_\alpha)$ where elements of $\mathcal{A}$ are called annotations and $\preceq_\alpha$ is a partial ordering on $\mathcal{A}$. aRDF further assumes that $\mathcal{A}$ has a unique bottom element. It can be shown that our predicate $\phi$, which serves as the annotation, satisfies the partial ordering requirement. If $\phi, \phi_1, \phi_2$ are non-null conjunctive predicates such that $\exists \phi_2 | (\phi \equiv \phi_1 \wedge \phi_2) = true$, then $\phi_1 \preceq_\alpha \phi$, else $\phi, \phi_1$ are incompatible. If the predicate $\phi$ is omitted, the *subset-of*$(X, Y, \phi)$ relationship defaults to *subset-of*$(X, Y, true)$. The $\preceq_\alpha$, thus defines a partial order over the set of predicates, with the top element *subset-of*$(X, Y, true)$. According to the aRDF principles, an *annotated RDF theory* (aRDF-theory for short) is a finite set of triples (r, p:a, v) where r is a resource name, p is a property name, a $\in \mathcal{A}$ and v is a value (which could also be a resource name) in dom(p).

An aRDF-interpretation $\mathcal{I}$ is a mapping from *Univ* to $\mathcal{A}$ where *Univ* is the set of all triples. An aRDF-interpretation $\mathcal{I}$ satisfies (r, p:a, v) iff a $\preceq_\alpha \mathcal{I}$(r, p, v). $\mathcal{I}$ satisfies an aRDF-theory $\mathcal{O}$ iff:

**(S1)** : $\mathcal{I}$ satisfies every $(\mathrm{r}, \mathrm{p}, \mathrm{v}) \in \mathcal{O}$.

**(S2)** : For all transitive properties $p \in P$ and for all $p$-paths $Q = \{t_1, \ldots t_k\}$ in $\mathcal{O}$, where $t_i = (r_i, p_i : a_i, r_{i+1})$, and $\forall a \in \mathcal{A}$ such that $a \preceq_\alpha a_i$ for all $1 < i < k$, it is the case that $a \preceq_\alpha I(r_1, p, r_{k+1})$.

Further, $\mathcal{O}$ is *consistent* iff there is at least one aRDF-interpretation that satisfies it, and $(\mathrm{r}, \mathrm{p:a}, \mathrm{v})$ entails $(\mathrm{r}, \mathrm{p:a}, \mathrm{v})$ iff every aRDF-interpretation that satisfies $\mathcal{O}$ also satisfies $(\mathrm{r}, \mathrm{p:a}, \mathrm{v})$. Udrea et al. [2010] prove that if the annotation $\mathcal{A}$ is a partial order with a top element, then any aRDF theory $\mathcal{O}$ is consistent. Since in our case, $\preceq_\alpha$ is a partial order with a top element, it is consistent as an appropriate annotation for aRDF.

Similar to the $\preceq_\alpha$ relationship, one can define the $\preceq_{po}$ relationship for all endurants that can be decomposed into parts and form a *part-of* partial order. We assume that the atomic parts that collectively constitute a larger endurant entity represent the finest granularity level that an application would need. It has been argued that *part-of* is a complex relationship that can lead to ambiguities if not interpreted properly. For example, if one says *(musician part-of orchestra)* and *(arm part-of musician)* then one should not infer *(arm part-of orchestra)* since the first use of *part-of* refers to a set membership and the latter user refers to a physical componenthood, and hence transitivity does not apply [Artale et al., 1996]. We therefore restrict the *part-of* to only physical (also called mereotopogical) componenthood[3] (see [Varzi, 1996] for the detailed axiomatic semantics related to parthood). This allows us to consider that a whole does not exist without its parts, and that parthood is a transitive relationship.

Several authors have developed theories for temporalizing the *subset-of* and the *part-of* relationships, so that one can make statements like *The followers of leader $N_1$ is a subset-of the members of party $P_1$ during interval $[t_1, t_2]$*. We treat each temporal shift in collection membership or parthood as events, and therefore do not need to treat them any differently.

## 2.3.5   THE SEMANTICS OF THE *SUBEVENT-OF* RELATIONSHIP

In the previous subsections, we have intuitively used the *subevent-of* relationship and specified a few of its properties in rules (2.1) and (2.2). In this subsection we take a closer look at the semantics of this relationship.

Let $\mathbf{E}$ be the set of all events and $\mathbf{D}$ be the set of all endurants. If $e_1, e_2 \in \mathbf{E}$, $e_2 \preceq_E e_1$ represents a direct subevent relationship, and $e_2 \preceq_E^+ e_1$ denotes all transitive subevent relationships. We use the notation $\preceq_E^+ (e_1)$ to refer to the set of all transitive descendants of $e_1$ (not including $e_1$ itself) along the $\preceq_E$ edge label. We can make the following observations about the $\preceq_E$ relationship.

1. If $e_1, e_2, e_3 \in \mathbf{E}$, and $e_3 \preceq_E e_1 \wedge e_3 \preceq_E e_2$, then $e_3.start \geq max(e_1.start, e_2.start)$ and $e_3.end \geq min(e_1.end, e_2.end)$

2. If $e_1, e_2 \in \mathbf{E}$, and $e_2 \preceq_E e_1$ then

---

[3]This means we do not cover propositions like "carbon is a part of steel" or "punctuality is a part of discipline."

(a) *contained-in($e_2$.located-in, $e_1$.located-in)* if $e_1$, $e_2$ have single geometry locations.

(b) *contained-in($e_2$.located-in, cover-of($e_1$.located-in))* if $e_1$ has a multi-geometry location and $e_2$ has a single-geometry location, where *cover-of* is a function that computes a single minimal polygon containing the geometries of $e_1$ – this can be a bounding box or a convex hull or some other application-specific function.

(c) *contained-in(cover-of($e_2$.located-in), cover-of($e_1$.located-in))* if $e_1$, $e_2$ have multi-geometry locations.

3. If $e_1$, $e_2$, $e_3 \in \mathbf{E}$, and $e_3 \preceq_E e_1 \wedge e_3 \preceq_E e_2$, then

(a) *contained-in($e_3$.located-in, $e_1$.located-in $\sqcap_s$ $e_2$.located-in)* if $e_1$, $e_2$, $e_3$ have single geometry locations and $\sqcap_s$ is the spatial intersection operation

(b) *contained-in($e_3$.located-in, cover-of($e_1$.located-in $\sqcap_s$ $e_2$.located-in))* if $e_1$ has a single geometry and $e_2$, $e_3$ have multiple geometry locations

(c) *contained-in(cover-of($e_3$.located-in), cover-of($e_1$.located-in $\sqcap_s$ $e_2$.located-in))* if $e_1$, $e_2$, $e_3$ have multiple geometry locations.

4. If $e_1$, $e_2 \in \mathbf{E}$, and $e_2 \preceq_E e_1$ then $gran_T(e_2) \preceq_T gran_T(e_1)$ where $gran_T(e)$ is the temporal granularity of event $e$.

5. If $e_1$, $e_2 \in \mathbf{E}$, and $e_2 \preceq_E e_1$ then $gran_S(e_2) \preceq_S gran_S(e_1)$ where $gran_S(e)$ is the spatial granularity of event $e$.

6. If $e_1$, $e_2$, $e_3 \in \mathbf{E}$, and $e_3 \preceq_E e_1 \wedge e_3 \preceq_E e_2$, $gran_T(e_3) \preceq_{TG} min(gran_T(e_1), gran_T(e_2))$ where $\preceq_{TG}$ means "having equal or finer temporal granularity."

7. If $e_1$, $e_2$, $e_3 \in \mathbf{E}$, and $e_3 \preceq_E e_1 \wedge e_3 \preceq_E e_2$, $gran_S(e_3) \preceq_{SG} min(gran_S(e_1), gran_S(e_2))$ where $\preceq_{SG}$ means "having equal or finer spatial granularity."

Let $\mathbf{R}$ be the set of all relationships, and $PR \subset \mathbf{R}$ be a subcategory of binary relationships that occur between endurants and perdurants. For example, *participates-in*(object, event), *agent-of*(person, action) are forms of $PR$. We now make two assertions with respect to the interaction between $PR$ relationships and the $\preceq_E$ relationship.

**Assertion 1** *If $p(o, e_0)$ is in $PR$, $o$ is a collection endurant of some type $T$, and $e_1 \preceq_E e_0$, then if $p(o', e_1)$ is valid where $o'$ is a collection of the same type $T$, then $o' \subseteq o$.*

In other words, the event participation relationships state that if one collection of some type participates in an event, then a second collection of the same type has the same relationship with its super-event, then the second collection is a superset of the first. Thus, the injured rally goers is a subset of the set of rally goers because the injury event is a subevent of the rally.

**Assertion 2** *If $p(o, e_1)$ is in $PR$, $o$ is a decomposable endurant, $o_p \in part\text{-}of^+(o)$, then*

1. $p(o_p, e_1) \Rightarrow p(o, e_1)$.

2. *Additionally, if $e_1 \preceq_E e_0$ and $p(o_{p'}, e_0)$ is valid where part-of$(o_{p'}, o)$ then part-of$(o_p, o_{p'})$ .*

The first clause states that if a part of an object participates in a relationship, we can infer that the whole object also participates in it. Assuming the connectedness of the object parts, the second clause says that if two parts of the same object participates in both an event and its superevent, then the part active in the subevent is a subpart of the part active in the superevent. For example, if the bumper of a car participates in an collision and the body of the same car partipates in the accident involving this collision (the accident involves other subevents like injury), then the bumper must be a part of this car.

## 2.3.6    THE SEMANTICS OF COLLECTIVE EVENTS

Next, we consider another category of events that we call *collective events*. Intuitively, a collective event is a bigger event formed by grouping a set of smaller *constituent events* because they are related along some attribute dimension(s). The formation of this collection is independent of any subevent relationships among the constituent events. Thus, if $e_1$, $e_2$ are two subevents of event $e_0$, and $e_1$ belongs to a collective event $ce_i$, there is no need for $e_0$ or $e_2$ to belong to $ce_i$. From our previous example, the "recent political unrest" of a country can be considered as a set of incidents of political unrest within a near-past time interval. Although some of these incidents are related by subevent or other relationships (e.g., `leads-to`), they are generally unconnected.

We can think of collective events as the result of a grouping operation on the event nodes of our graph structured event database. Let $\mathbf{E}$ be a set of event instances (i.e., event nodes) in the database. Let $\phi(\mathbf{E})$ be an event selecting query where the selection predicates in $\phi(.)$ are specified on the domains, ranges, and labels of edges outgoing from $\mathbf{E}$. If $\mathbf{E}'$ is the result of the query, and $L_g$ is the set of edge labels that occur in the outgoing edges of nodes $\mathbf{E}'$, we can define a collective event node $E_C$ in the following ways:

- create node $E_C$ and map it to the nodes of $\mathbf{E}'$ through a *has-member* (inverse, *member-of*) relationship; in this case $E_C$, whose properties are given by the union of edge labels in $L_g$, outgoing from the member events of $E_C$. The temporal and spatial extents of $E_C$ are given by the same rules that determine the extents in the case of the subevent relationships.

- define a partition function $\pi(.)$ over nodes $\mathbf{E}'$ along edge labels $L_g' \subset L_g$, such that $\pi(.)$ partitions the nodes of into groups $E_{C_1}, \ldots E_{C_k}$, where $k$ is the number of unique value combinations of the edge ranges outgoing from $\mathbf{E}'$ having labels in $L_g'$. These groups, $E_{C_1}, \ldots E_{C_k}$ will be collective event nodes themselves. A collective event node $E_C$ is defined such that each node $E_{C_i}$ has a *subcollection-of* relationship to $E_C$. The inclusion of the partition function generalizes the previous case where there is only one partition.

- Recall that our basic event model derives from RDF. Therefore, in our model any edge label (i.e., the property of a node) $l$ may have subproperties $l_1, \ldots l_m$. If each of the $m$ subproperties of $l$ are included in $L_g$, the set of common labels, one can naturally construct a collective event $E_L$ over $l$, which can have finer collective events over its $m$ subproperties. As before, each collective event over subproperty $l_i$ has a *subcollection-of* relationship to event $E_L$.

Note that the formation of collective events is not exactly the same as the GROUP BY operation of SQL and SPARQL which produces a partition of a set based on the values of a set of grouping attributes and is accompanied by an aggregate function on a non-grouping attribute for each partition. **EXAMPLE: The Newsan Database of Political Unrest.** Newsan is monitoring the recent spread of unrest by a number of insurgent groups in TroubleCountry, and would like to put this information on a web site. It queries the event database for all event nodes whose `rdf:type` matches the concepts "violence," "protest" or "demonstration" or their subclasses. The results of this query are presented in Table 2.3, where each triple represents an event node or parts of its 2-neighborhood. If both

| Table 2.3: Three violent events and their neighborhoods. | | |
|---|---|---|
| event-100 rdf:type bombing | event-200 rdf:type burning | event-300 rdf:type demonstration |
| event-100 located-at Town1 | event-200 located-at Town2 | event-300 located-at Town1 |
| Town1 located-in County1 | Town2 located-in County1 | event-300 occurs_during TR3 |
| event-100 occurs_during TR1 | event-200 occurs_during TR2 | TR3 occurs-before(3hours) TR1 |
| event-100 damages B1 | event-200 affects C2 | event-300 led-by Party2 |
| B1 rdf:type police-station | C2 rdf:type city-hall | Party2 has-leader P1 |
| event-100 claimed-by O1 | event-200 claimed-by O1 | P1 associates-with O2 |
| O1 has-name BadGroup1 | | O2 has-name BadGroup2 |
| O1 subclass-of separatist | | O2 subclass-of banned-party |

"burning" and "bombing" are subclasses of "violence," then one can construct a collective event called "violent events in County1." Similarly, it is possible to define collective events "violent events claimed by BadGroup1" and "Unrest in Town1."

## 2.3.7   MODELING CONSTRUCTS FOR EVENTS

We have seen earlier in the chapter that several event-to-event relationships carry specific semantics. For example, the subevent relationship implies temporal containment. We conclude this chapter with an outline of other, more general, modeling considerations for events and inter-event relationships beyond the specific relationships discussed so far in this chapter. While we have considered the $E^*$ event model as an RDF-style graph-based model, many of the general conceptual modeling principles apply.

**Disjointedness.** A set of events (or event categories) can be declared to be completely disjoint, spatially disjoint, temporally disjoint, or spatiotemporally disjoint, causally disjoint and so forth. Political rallies are spatially disjoint from State Assembly meetings; the Winter session of the State Assembly and all their subevents are temporally disjoint from those of the Fall session; birth and death of any entity are completely disjoint.

**Coverage.** Coverage is the constraint that states that a larger event must be composed of $k$ smaller events and nothing else. The subevent relationship does not always imply coverage but several applications can declare a coverage constraint over its set of subevents. Coverage does not automatically imply disjointedness, but in many cases subevents can be covering and disjoint. Many "structured" events such as weddings have distinct phases of a ritual structure of subevents: all of which must occur for the larger event to complete.

**Ordering.** A set of events may be declared to be (partially) ordered along some axis. For example, the subevent relationship does not normally imply an ordering amongst the children of a parent event, but an application may declare that a certain subevent relationship signature (consisting of the domain of the relationship, the relationship label, the range of the relationship along with constraints on the domain and the range) must be ordered. In our previous example, one can state that any event node $e$ in the *subevent-of* tree under (and including) the "wedding" event has the property that children of $e$ will be totally ordered by time interval (i.e., the time intervals of two consecutive events will not overlap). This constraint will hold when the user creates instances of events for the "wedding" event, and the user will have to respect the order of the child events. Ordering can also be the property of other relationships. For example, one can have the constraint: "for events $e_1, e_2, causes(e_1, e_2) \implies follows(e_2, e_1)$."

**LifeSpan and SpaceSpan.** As Artale et al. [2010] point out for temporary entities, events may also have constraints on their the length of their lifetime or the largest locality where they may occur or some combination of both. For example, one can state that a Party Convention will last only three days; the CIDR conference only occurs in Asilomar, California; no two consecutive SIGMOD conferences will occur in the same location. Similar constraints may also be placed on frequencies with which instances of a class of events may occur – an annual conference will take place once a year.

**Graph Pattern Constraints.** A more general class of constraints can be specified in terms of the graph patterns. Consider a complex constraint like "The same participant cannot participate in three consecutive subevents of event type $e_X$." Such a constraint can be modeled in the E* framework by giving the pattern $P_1$ as follows, and then stating such a pattern cannot be instantiated.

```
(e1, e2, e3) subevent-of e0
(e0, e1, e2, e3) subclass-of-or-self eX
e2 follows e1
e3 follows e2
p1 participates in (e1, e2)
p2 participates in (e2, e3)
p1 same-as p2
```

where `same-as` implies that the p1, p2 resolve to the same entity. We will present examples of several such constraints in subsequent chapters.

CHAPTER 3

# Implementing an Event Data Model

In the previous chapter, we presented an ontology based event model, and we looked at the generic properties of events and their formal properties. In this chapter we will explore how event information can be declared to an event-based information system and how this declaration can be translated to a storage scheme. We will first consider the case where the event information can be described through an ontology based schema. We assume the readers' familiarity with the extended Entity Relationship (EER) model and the transformation of that model into a relational model (see, for example, [Elmasri and Navathe, 1994]). We will follow a similar path and draw comparisons with the EER family of models (including several temporal versions of the EER model) and the translation scheme to illustrate how an event model will be different from a EER style modeling scheme. We will consider transforming the same event model to a couple of different storage schemes. Next, we will consider schemaless semistructured event descriptions and their transformation into a storage scheme.

## 3.1 AN EXTENDED ENTITY RELATIONSHIP MODEL FOR STRUCTURED EVENTS

Event schemata can be declared for event categories that have some well defined structure and does not have event instances that fall outside this structure. A typical category of events that fall within this restriction are scheduled events, i.e., events for which a schedule can be created. For example, a prototypical conference has a fairly structured series of events, and thus can be declared through an event schema. On the other hand, perhaps a day in the park cannot be described through a rigid event schema and must be modeled in a semistructured manner.

Let us consider a simple EER style schema to describe conferences as shown in Figure 3.1. In this schema, more than one session is part of a conference. A session can be a keynote session, paper session or a demo session, which are mutually exclusive. A paper can be presented only at one session. Papers have authors who are persons. Further, every author has an author position in a paper. To add spatiotemporal constraints to this model, one can specify additional constraints such as (a) the location of a session is spatially inside the location of the same conference, (b) the date of a session is within the start and end dates of the same conference, (c) the order of a paper in a session is an integer starting from 1, and incremented by 1 (i.e., there is no skipped integer), and so forth. However, these constraints must be specified per entity or relationship because there is

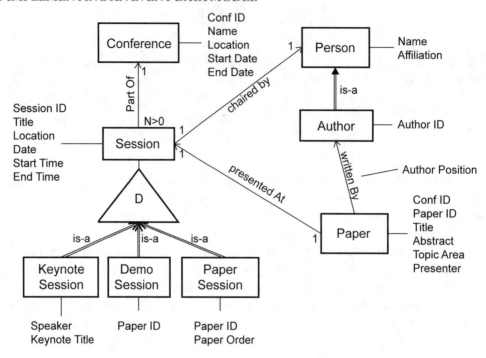

**Figure 3.1:** A traditional EER model for a conference. The double-shaft arrows represent the is-a relationship (specialization) supported by the EER model.

no built-in way of capturing them in the EER modeling paradigm. Let us now add some explicit temporal constructs to this model. Combi et al. [2008] introduced a set of temporal constraints on top of the TIME-ER model of Gregersen [2006]. Since the (Conf ID, Paper ID) attribute-pair for the Paper entity is time invariant and cannot be reassigned to another paper at a later time, it can be declared as a **temporal key**. For each Session entity, one can define a **lifespan** in terms of the date, the start time and end time attributes of the entity. This specifies that the session entity exists within the interval of its lifespan. We can also declare that the *isa* relationship between Session and the Keynote, Paper and Demo Sessions is a **temporally disjoint subclass-superclass relationship** such that an instance of Session can be a member of only one of its subclasses at all instants of time. Once these constraints are specified, one would ideally be able *autogenerate* a set of additional constraints on the date and time stamps; additionally, one should be able to autogenerate the code to enforce these constraints. Transforming the EER model to relational tables according to standard tasks, we can obtain the following schema (we discarded the Person entity but preserved its properties).

```
Conferences(confID, name, location, startDate, endDate)
Sessions(confID, sessionID, title, location, date, startTime, endTime)
Keynotes(confID, sessionID, speaker, keynoteTitle)
PaperSessions(confID, sessionID, paperID, paperOrder)
```

```
Demos(confID, sessionID, paperID)
Papers(confID, sessionID, paperID, title, abstract, topicArea, presenter)
Authors(authorID, name, affiliation)
AuthorPaper(authorID, confID, paperID, authorPosition)
SessionChairs(confID, sessionID, name, affiliation)
```

Let us now attempt to map the constraints to this relational schema using first order statements.

1. The location of a session is inside the location of the conference.

   ```
   Sessions(confID, sessionID, _, sLocation, _, _, _), Conferences(confID,
   _, cLocation, _, _) ⇒
   inside(sLocation, cLocation)
   ```

2. The lifespan of a session is temporally contained in the lifespan of a conference.

   ```
   Sessions(confID, sessionID, _, _, date, startTime, endTime),
   Conferences(confID, _, _, startDate, endDate) ⇒ Sessions.date ≥
   Conferences.startDate
   Sessions(confID, sessionID, _, _, date, startTime, endTime),

   Conferences(confID, _, _, startDate, endDate) ⇒ Sessions.date ≤
   Conferences.endDate
   ```

3. Temporal disjointedness constraint.

   ```
   Sessions(confID1, sessionID1, _, _, date1, startTime1, endTime1),
   Keynotes(confID1, sessionID1, _, _) Sessions(confID1, sessionID2, _,
   _, date1, startTime2, endTime2), Demos(confID1, sessionID2, _)⇒ ¬
   TOverlaps([startTime1, endTime1], [startTime2, endTime2])
   ```

   The temporal disjointedness clause captures the fact that a demo session, and a keynote session occurring on the same date in a conference will not temporally overlap. The *TOverlaps* function is assumed to accept two intervals and return a Boolean result. Similar constraints can be imposed for the paper sessions and the keynote sessions.

The first constraint demonstrates the need to create a new set of facts `within(location1, location2)` that is not in the model itself. If the RDBMS supports spatial data types, this can be modeled by creating a view over both relations and using a trigger to check the *within* constraint through a spatial function. However, if the location is specified only as a name (e.g., the name of a conference room where the session is held), one cannot use a spatial function. In contrast, having the ability to treat the constraint as a tuple generator for the *within* relation leads to the creation of new knowledge (assertions) as a by-product of the constraint. That means, using the constraint, we can create a new relation `within(spatial_entity, spatial_entity)` and populate it with tuples like `within('Ballroom B', 'Hotel Coronado')`. The other constraints demonstrate the need to have multi-table constraints – which cannot be directly modeled in a standard relational DBMS, but it needs a more complex implementation involving insert triggers. Insert triggers can check, for example, that a new demo sessionID can be inserted in the demo table if and only if there is no such sessionID in the Keynotes or PaperSessions table entries related to the same conference. Alternately, we can define queries corresponding to the constraints that must always evaluate to true, (or false as the case may be) and every update must execute these queries to verify a valid database state. In either case, the automatic generation of constraints that should be implicit in the event model can be quite involved if we assume a standard relational implementation of the event model.

In our model so far, we have not expressed all the constraints related to the sessions. Suppose we want to model the fact that sessions are divided into four session groups morning, pre-lunch, post-lunch, post-coffee and that sessions within each group occur concurrently, while any morning session will precede a pre-lunch session. Further, the last day of the conference may or may not have the last two sessions. To model these characteristics, we need to define **temporal grouping** and **concurrency (and precedence) constraints** of events in a relational setting. Notice that our intention is to *declare* the groups, and not to compute them from data as part of a group-by query. We are not in a position to specify the exact time slots when these sessions will occur because they will differ for every conference. We can however say that the morning session will occur before the pre-lunch session which occur before the post-lunch session etc., and we can say that all sessions within a session group will start and end at the same time. One rational way of making these declarations is to create a new attribute called sessionGroup for the Sessions table, and restrict its possible values to the enumerated set {morning, pre-lunch, post-lunch, post-coffee}, and then add single-table and multi-table constraints like the following:

```
Sessions(confID, sessionID1, _, _, 'morning', date, startTime1, endTime1),
Sessions(confID, sessionID2, _, _, 'morning', date, startTime2, endTime2) ⇒
startTime1 = startTime2, endTime1 = endTime2


Sessions(confID, sessionID1, _, _, 'morning', date, startTime1, endTime1),
Sessions(confID, sessionID2, _, _, 'pre-lunch', date, startTime2, endTime2)
⇒ endTime1 < startTime2


Conferences(confID, _, _, startDate, endDate), Sessions(confID, sessionID,
_, _, sessionGroup, date, startTime1, endTime1), Conferences.endDate =
Sessions.date ⇒ sessionGroup ≠ 'post-lunch'
```

The first is a concurrency constraint, the second is a temporal precedence constraint and the third is an denial constraint to encode impossible database states. If in addition, we want to create new subclasses of the Session entity called morningSession, preLunchSession etc., we can create these subclasses through a set of view on the Sessions table with the sessionGroup table restricted to the value 'morning', 'pre-lunch', etc. Note that in this implementation, the temporal grouping is implicitly encoded, not declaratively specified because standard relational modeling schemes do not allow it.

The above examples illustrate that it is *possible* to construct a schematized event system using a standard relational platform; however, a number of domain constraints that are "natural" to event descriptions must be defined at the level of an application.

## 3.2    A PATTERN-BASED APPROACH TO STRUCTURED EVENTS

Recently, Scherp et al. [2009a] introduced a model of representing events based on a set of *patterns*. The basic premise of this model, called $F$, derives from the $E$ model of Westermann and Jain [2007]. The basic premise of this model is that an event model must have the basic primitives to allow the following "aspects" of events.

1. **Participation of objects in events.** Representing participation of living and non-living objects such as people, animals, and other material objects in events and the roles they play in events.

2. **Temporal duration of events.** As events unfold over time, their temporal duration needs to be modeled. This can be conducted using absolute or relative representations of points in time.

3. **Spatial extension of objects.** Similarly, objects unfold over space. Thus, modeling their spatial extension needs to be supported. This can be also modeled using absolute or relative positioning.

4. **Structural relationships between events.** There are three kinds of structural relationships between events, namely (a) mereological, (b) causal, and (c) correlation relationships. The mereological relationship reflect how events are made up of other events and is identical to the *subevent-of* relationship we described in the last chapter. Causal relationships require the modeling of causes and effects and should support the integration and use of different causal theories. Correlation refers to two events that may or may not have a common cause; however, unlike causality, event correlation is typically easy to observe and record.

5. **Annotability of events.** Annotability (called "Documentation" by the authors) refers to the ability to associate an arbitrary number of auxiliary information items to any event. These annotations could be additional metadata, media evidences, or documents that provide additional information that cannot be determined at schema development time.

6. **Event interpretations.** Relationships between events such as causality and correlation can be matter of subjectivity and interpretation. Therefore, an event model should provide the ability to associate relationships with further descriptors (e.g., attributes) that are not properties of the event or objects but can act as additional qualifiers to the relationships.

Interestingly, for each of these "aspects," the model proposes a pattern, which is a UML-style prototype that would be tailored to fit the specific application model, although not every pattern is needed for every application. One clear benefit of using UML patterns is that the techniques of mapping them to a relational database are well understood. At the same time, the model has a strong ontological foundation; it specializes a version of the DOLCE-Lite and the DNS (Descriptions and Situations) ontologies, and uses these terms to define entity categories and relationships that are used in defining the UML patterns. In these notes, we explain three of these patterns and leave it to the readers to explore the rest.

Figure 3.2 shows the UML pattern for a typical participation.

This model requires every participation process to be explicitly defined in terms of the events and objects that partake in the process. In the conference example, one can consider "giving a talk" as a kind of participation that occurs within a session, which will be the "DescribedEvent" and can be modeled as a part of a larger "situation," with the idea that other events might also be part of the same participation situation. The parameter `LocationParameter` describes the general spatial region where the objects are located. It "parametrizes" a `SpaceRegion` and defines a property `isParameterFor` to the `Participant` role. The `Object` that is classified by the `Participant` has a `Quality` with the property `hasRegion` of a `SpaceRegion`. Thus, using the `LocationParameter`, we can define the location(s) represented by `SpaceRegions` that are relevant for describing the event in a given context.

A more complex pattern is the merology pattern shown in 3.3 which models how subevents can be composed into a larger event. In this model, the "component" is an event that is assimilated into the

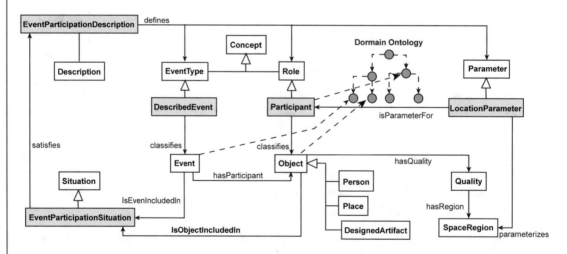

**Figure 3.2:** The participation pattern of the F model. The white rectangles represent concepts in the DOLCE Ultra-light and DnS ontologies. The colored rectangles are specializations created by the F model (the arrows with broad arrowheads represent the subclass relationship). The other arrows are directional – the tail of the arrow represents the domain of the property while the head represents the range. The dashed arrows are ontology references. Not shown in the figure is an additional time parameter (just like the location parameter) which depicts the time of the participation.

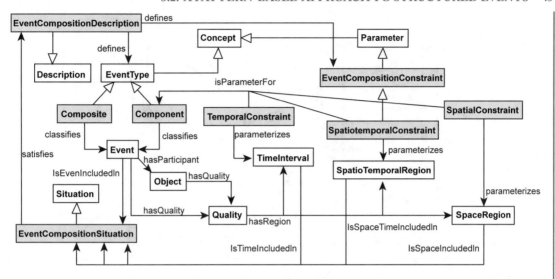

**Figure 3.3:** The merology pattern of the F model. This figure does not show some of the event related associations shown in Fig. 3.2. The convention of the colored and white rectangles is the same as in Figure 3.2.

composite event. In a conference example, a conference session can be modeled as a set of talks (i.e., components) while each talk can be further composed of a presentation component followed by a question-answer component. Formally, an EventCompositionSituation includes one instance of an event that is classified by the concept Composite and many events classified as its Component(s). Accordingly, an EventCompositionSituation satisfies a CompositionDescription that defines the concepts Composite and Component for classifying the composite event and its component events. Events that play the Component role may be further qualified by temporal, spatial, and spatiotemporal constraints. As events are formally defined as entities that exist in time and not in space, constraints including spatial restrictions are expressed through the objects participating in the component event. For instance, a Component event may be required to occur within a certain time-interval. Any such constraints are formally expressed by one or multiple instances of the EventCompositionConstraint. They define qualifying values for temporal, spatial, and spatiotemporal qualities of a component event as shown in Figure 3.3. Thus, with the composition pattern, events may be arbitrarily temporally related to each other, i.e., they might be disjoint, overlapping, or otherwise ordered. The temporal constraints have been discussed in the previous section.

The causality pattern shown in Figure 3.4 defines two EventTypes called Cause and Effect which classify Events. It further defines a Description of the causal relationship between these events, which is classified by a Justification. Thus, the pattern explicitly expresses the causal relationship between the cause and the effect under the justification of some theory. A theory might

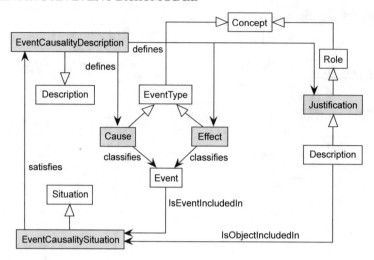

**Figure 3.4:** The causality pattern of the F model.

be an opinion, a scientific law, or a chain of reasoning. However, in many application scenarios the justification may not be necessary. For example, in a conference setting, the questions and answers can be viewed as causes and effects, but it may not have the need for a justification.

To implement this pattern-based conceptual model, the authors have expressed the model in RDF/OWL[1] and implemented it as an application interface on top of Sesame, an RDF store [Scherp et al., 2009b].

## 3.3    A HYBRID APPROACH FOR STRUCTURED AND SEMI-STRUCTURED EVENTS

Perry [2008] presents a different strategy for implementing an ontological event model. It decomposes the data representation problem into two parts – the first part is a pure RDF model that does not need any special handling of data types, and the second part is based on abstract data types, which have a structure but must be accessed through methods. There are many alternative implementations of the first part. The simplest technique is to use an unnormalized triple store. A more complex technique would normalize the triple-centric semantic model into a set of tables and implement inferencing procedures on this structure. Heymans et al. [2008] present an excellent overview of the process based on IBM's Minerva system. The second part is created on top of an object-relational system so that important data types like time and location can be modeled as tables with additional methods to facilitate the computation of functions like `overlaps` among tempo-

---

[1]available at http://www.uni-koblenz-landau.de/koblenz/fb4/AGStaab/Research/ontologies/events/model.owl/view

```
Dynamic_Entity ⊏ Continuent
Named_Place ⊏ Continuent
Spatial_Occurrent ⊏ Occurrent
Nonspatial_Occurrent ⊏ Occurrent
Spatial_Region ⊏ Entity
Named_Place ⊏ ∃located_at[tₛ, tₑ].Spatial_Region
Spatial_Occur
```

**Figure 3.5:** Upper Ontology of Perry's Model written in Description Logic. The ⊏ symbol represents the subclass relationship.

ral intervals or spatial regions. This generic strategy can be used for the implementation of both structured and semi-structured event models.

The basic premise of Perry's implementation scheme is to model events along the spatial, temporal, and thematic axes, thus modeling events as a spatiotemporal-thematic entity without any of the event-specific properties we described in Section 2.3. Like the F model in the previous section, Perry's model consists of an upper ontology as shown in Figure 3.5, which uses timestamps on valid time intervals for time-dependent relationships (like `located_at`). The properties of the `Spatial_Region` entity is obtained from a GIS ontology and contains geographic entities like points, lines, and polygons. This choice is motivated by the desire to map the "normal" RDF data to a triple store, and then directly map the spatial data to an existing object-relational database. A side effect of this choice is that the topological relationships between spatial regions (like `inside`, `overlaps` etc.) can be specified in the RDF model, but the implementation directly maps to the corresponding methods for computing these relationships, provided by the underlying DBMS. In the same spirit, the temporal constructs specified in the RDF part of the model uses the entities from the OWL-Time ontology [Hobbs and Pan, 2004], but the timestamps are mapped to datetime data types within a relational system such that relationships like `before` can be transformed into data procedures at query time. Thus, the relational equivalent of Perry's model can be viewed as the following schema, which is based on Oracle's documentation of their semantic data store.

```
RDFValues(id, URI)
RDFTriples(triple_id, subject_id, property_id, object_id, triple_type,
isBidirectional, parent_triple_id)
InferredTriples(triple_id, subject_id, property_id, object_id, ...)
TemporalTriples(triple_id, subject_id, property_id, object_id, start_date,
end_date)
SpatialData(value_id, shape, rdf_serialization)
```

A few issues should be observed in this implementation.

- The first table creates a dictionary for RDF URIs.

- The second and the third tables are nearly identical except that the third table is created by computing all inference rules that apply to the semantic model. The `TemporalTriples` table is very similar to the `RDFTriples` table except that it stores the valid time interval associated with the triples. This example illustrates how "edge properties" (recall our discussion of the aRDF model [Udrea et al., 2010] in Section 2.3.2) can be encoded in a relational setting. The `SpatialData` stores the spatial information including the geometry and a spatial index for more efficient computation of spatial operations.

- The `triple_type` attribute provides special status to some triples. For example, a triple with `rdf:type` is special because it relates instances to their classes. A parent triple $p$ of a triple $t$ is a triple such $t$ is an instantiation of $p$ because $t$'s subject (resp. object) may be a subtype of $p$'s subject (resp. object) and $t$'s property may be a subproperty of $p$'s property.

- The inference rules include the standard RDF entailment rules, as well as any domain specific rules that are defined for an application domain. Thus, in our conference example, the rule that a session location must be "inside" the conference location will be executed and a new triple like (`'BallRoom B' inside 'Coronado Hotel'`) will be materialized in the `InferredTriples` table. Similarly, the entailment rules for events specified in the previous chapter can be implement through the rule engine.

## 3.4 AN IMPLEMENTATION SCHEME FOR E*

### 3.4.1 DECLARING E* EVENTS WITH E*ML

In the last chapter, we presented the conceptual model of E* and described a number of different modeling constructs along with their semantics. Here, we revisit the model specification problem from an implementation standpoint, and we present a concrete data definition language we call E*ML that will allow a user to express E* constructs. Recall that in the last chapter, we used an RDF-inspired graph-like representation for events. While E*ML is strongly influenced by the modeling constructs of RDF, it is more "structured" compared to RDF, but it retains many salient features of RDF, and it can be viewed as a graph. Similar standard data definition languages like SQL DDL, and RDFS the E* Modeling Language (E*ML) specifies entities, relationships, and constraints[2]. Like XML Schema, it specifies that certain properties are optional. We present the salient features of the E*ML language using examples. It should be simple to see that this model maps directly to the RDF-like model presented in the last section, but we leave it to the readers to validate this claim.

**Basics.** E*ML admits standard scalar data types – integer, float, string, dateTime, . . ., the temporal data type timeInterval, geometric data types like point and polygon, and media types like image, audio, and video (which are associated with standard media formats). On these basic types, E*ML allows the following data constructors:

---

[2]RDFS does not allow constraints.

(a) `enum` – for enumerating a set of possible values of a variable,

(b) `set` – an unordered collection of similar values,

(c) `list` – an ordered collection of similar values,

(d) `timeSeries` – a list that uses dateTime or ordered timeInterval as its index,

(e) `union` – a choice over any one of a set of types,

(f) `tuple` – the cross product of different data types, and

(g) `graph` – a node and edge labeled graph that may or may not be connected. In the following, we will build the event model in E*ML by composing these data types and constructors.

**Open Types.** We start by introducing the idea of *open types*, borrowed from the Asterix data model [Behm et al., 2011] of semistructured information. An *open type record* is a tuple data type where an instance of the type must respect the attributes and relationships declared in the type definition; however, an instance may also contain additional attributes and relationships that are not specified in the type declaration. This means that E*ML is not a strongly typed language. But it guarantees a flexibility that will be useful to record arbitrary events. A type could also be closed; in this case, the semantics of a type is identical to the data types we are familiar with. Thus, the data type `address` declared as

```
type address(
street_address string,
street_name string,
city string,
state string,
country string,
postal_code string
)
```

is a closed type, whereas system-defined data type `event` declared as

```
open type event::subClass*(DOLCE::perdurant)(
event_id integer,
occurs_during timeInterval,
occurs_at Location multiple optional,
observed_by union(Person, ImageDevice) multiple optional,
experienced_with Media multiple optional
)
```

is an open type. The event data type is the root type for all events. Notice in this declaration that (a) the `event` is derived from the ontology and can be any subclass of the class called `perdurant` in the DOLCE ontology and will thus inherit their properties; (b) `timeInterval` is a built-in data type; (c) an event is not required to have a location, but it can have one or more locations (e.g., location = "our favorite street corner" and location = a GPS-coordinate); (d) an event may have zero or more observers, and may be captured through zero or more media objects like images or video; (e) the `experienced_with` property has the data type Media, which is an abstraction over multiple imaging/audio devices that capture media information from the scene of an event.

To illustrate the "openness" of the open type, let us first declare a subtype of the main `event` type called `political_rally`.

```
open type political_rally::DOLCE::activity(
called_by subClass*(DOLCE::agentive-social-object),
speaker union(DOLCE::social-person, DOLCE::natural-person) multiple,
attended_by set(union(DOLCE::social-person, DOLCE::natural-person))
)
```

In this type, we see that the `political_rally` type is a specialized kind of event because it inherits from `activity`, which is a subtype of `event`; the multivalued `speaker` property has a domain represented by the union of two ontological concepts. The `attended-by` property is declared to be a set, whose members are either natural people (e.g., "John Fernandez") or social people (e.g., "union leader of X factory"). However, it is not expected that every attendee of the rally will be enumerated for any instance of the `political_rally`. Therefore, the use of the `set` allows us to specify additional attributes like `minCardinality` and `minCardinality` without having to instantiate all members of the set.

We now create an instance of the violent political rally described in Section 2.3.1. Let us assume that `NamedLocation` is a subtype of `Location` which can be identified by a name.

```
TroubleTownRally(type=political_rally, event_id=5,
occurs_during=(9/12/2010:14:00:00, 9/12/2010:17:00:00),
occurs_at=namedLocation(''TroubleTown''), called_by=''EthnicMinority,''
speaker=''EthnicLeader1,'' speaker=''EthnicLeader2,''
attended_by=set(set_id=$A19), condemned_by=newspaperEditorial(document_id=29345),
reaction_to=governmentDeclarationEvent(event_id=376)).
```

The last two properties link this instance of the rally event to a newspaper editorial and to another event of type `governmentDeclarationEvent` although the generic `political_rally` data type does not have these properties. Since the properties `condemned_by` and `reaction_to` are not known at the schema level, but only as part of an instance, the E*ML model treats them as properties private to the instance. Therefore, if there is another occurrence of the `reaction_to` property that does not have the same domain and range as this instance, E*ML will not consider it to be a violation.

One consequence of having open types is that data instances defined through E*ML are not strongly typed. That means although every instance belongs to exactly one minimal type, it is not the case that the properties of the instances are ascribed only through this minimal type. However, since E*ML does not support multiple inheritance, an instance will not have conflicting properties. If an instance $i_T$ of type $T$ inherits a property $p$, and the user defines a property $p'$ for $i_T$, such that the it violates some constraint that prohibits $p$ and $p'$ to be assigned to the same instance, the system will not accept the user-defined property $p'$. However, the system will not flag an error if two instances $i_T$ and $i_{T'}$ both have a property named $p$ even if these properties have the same signature because by the semantics of E*ML, they are treated as two distinct properties.

**Parameterized Properties and Subproperties.** In Section 2.3, we modeled temporal relationships by modeling them as RDF sentences having `start_time` and `end_time` properties. E*ML adopts a more general approach to the problem by allowing parameterized relationships, together with constraints that capture the semantics of the parameterization. Let us first consider the relationship `participates_in` whose domain is any person or group (i.e., union(DOLCE::agentive-social-object, DOLCE::natural-person) and range is event. We intend to express the relationship that an instance of this domain participates in the event for a period of time which must be between the lifespan of the event. In E*ML, we express this as the following:

```
open relationship participates_in(
domain union(DOLCE::agentive-social-object, DOLCE::natural-person),
range event,
inverse has_participant,
parameter participation_time list(timeInterval)
constraint not(timeInterval.overlaps({participation_time}),
constraint timeInverval.contained_in(domain.participation_time,
range.occurs_during)
)
```

This declaration introduces a second way of specifying relationships, and it is used when (a) the domain of the relationship is not modeled directly for an application, and (b) the relationship has additional properties such as the temporal parameter in this example. The constraint states that the participation time is a list of time intervals, i.e., a social object (or natural person) can participate in an event at several different time intervals; this list of time intervals must be non-overlapping, and it must be in temporally within the boundaries of the event forming the range of the relationship. The specification `timeInterval.contained_in` ensures that the `contained_in` function is interpreted in the context of the appropriate data type. The example also illustrates that relationships can be "open" in the same sense that types can be open. Let us now add one more constraint to the `participates_in` relationship to express the condition "if a person participates in an event, then during the participation, the location of the person will be within the location of the event." Let us assume that a natural person is simply declared as the following:

```
open type person::subClass*(union(DOLCE::social-person,
DOLCE:natural-person))(
person_id integer,
name string,
affiliation string multiple optional
)
```

Since the `person` type inherits from the ontology, it has a property called `e-temporal-location` that maps the location of the person to a temporal region, but there are no constraints on it. To express the above constraint in E*ML, we specialize (i.e., create a subproperty of) the `participates_in` relationship in the following way:

```
open relationship person_participates_in:participates_in(
domain person,
```

```
constraint location.contained_in(domain.e-temporal-location, range.occurs_at)
)
```

so that the constraint is applied only to `person` instances who take part in the `person_participates_in` relationship. The constraints associated with relationships can also be declared to have side effects; specifically, they may add properties to instances of an open type that serves as the domain or the range of the relationship. For example, consider the relationship causes between two events, as we saw in Section 3.2.

```
open relationship causes(
domain event,
range event,
constraint(timeInterval.before(domain.occurs_during, range.occurs_during))
constraint(addProperty(range, ''causal_explanation,'' text))
)
```

This constraint adds a property called `causal_explanation` to the range of the `causes` relationship (i.e., to the "effect event") – this is a text-valued data property. The additional property is added only to those event instances that take part in the `causes` relationship. This tuple-generating constraint takes advantage of the open type property of events, and yet avoids the burden of declaring this property for every single "effect event" at insertion time.

Next, we declare temporal disjointedness, temporal precedence and temporal concurrency constraints as discussed in Section 3.1. We define the event called `session`.

```
open type session::event(
session_id integer,
session_name integer,
...
subevent_of event multiple optional
constraint not(timeInterval.overlaps({subevent_of.range})) )
```

The constraint in this declaration specifies the set of all events that are `subevent_of` session, and ensures their temporal disjointedness. Finally, we present the structure of the `subevent-of` relationship that has been extensively discussed in Section 2.3.5. Recall our earlier discussions on granularity of time and locational information. In the following, we assume that granularity levels are represented as explicit properties of the `timeInterval` and `location` data types – thus, time (and timeInterval) can be presented at the granularity levels of years, months, days, hours and minutes.

```
open relationship subevent_of(
domain event;
range event;
constraint timeInverval.contained_in(domain.occurs_during,
range.occurs_during)
constraint location.contained_in(domain.occurs_at, range.occurs_at)
constraint domain.occurs_during.timeGranularity <=
range.occurs_during.timeGranularity
```

```
constraint domain.occurs_at.spatialGranularity <=
range.occurs_at.spatialGranularity
constraint subset_of(domain.participates_in.domain,
range.participates_in.domain)
)
```

The last constraint captures Assertion 1 on page 33. We did not place Assertion 2 in this specification because it applies to the parthood relationship of endurants rather than the `subevent_of` relationship.

**Quantification over Temporal and Spatial Domains.** In Sections 2.3.2 (resp. 2.3.3), we described universally, existentially and numerically quantified occurrence relations between a perdurant and its time (resp. location) of occurrence. For events, we use the properties `occurs_sometime_during` (resp. `occurs_somewhere_at`) to designate existential quantification. Normally, the existential quantification implies that the exact time interval of the event's occurrence is not known, but it is known to be with the specified lower and upper bounds. The E*ML language allows a single event to have both a universally quantified and an existentially quantified time of occurrence. The intended use is that an event can `occur_during` one time interval and `occur_sometime_during` another time interval, provided the duration of the latter is longer than the duration of the former. A speech event, for example, will occur_during the "talk session's" lifespan, but it will `occur_sometime_during` a speaker's work hours. Similar arguments hold if the location of the event is existentially quantified.

**Continuous Events.** An event is *continuous* (or *evolving*) when for every unit interval of a longer time interval, the event has a recorded "value" for a state measuring variable. As a special case, a continuous event can have *state variables* that change with both time and location. The development of a thunderstorm, characterized by the spatiotemporal change of a collection of state variables like air temperature, air pressure, wind velocity, precipitation, etc., can be modeled as a continuous event. However, state variables in a continuous event do not have to be numeric. In E*ML, we model a continuous event based on a specially designated variable called a **state_event**. Simply put, a state_event is an event that has a special parameter called `state`, which itself is modeled as a list of attribute-value pairs. A temporal continuous event is a `timeSeries` of `state_event` instances where the time is ordered by increasing and non-overlapping intervals. A spatiotemporal event is modeled as a `timeSeries` over a `set` of `state_event` instances such that each member of the set has an associated location and the set represents all `state_event` instances occurring at multiple locations during that time interval.

Let us revisit the example of the violent rally, and the evolving situation where the crowd turns violent and starts destroying property. Table 3.1 shows a part of the instance records reflecting the evolving situation. The event instance is a subevent of the `TroubleTownRally` event, and it shows four non-contiguous time intervals over which the events are reported. The model allows this non-contiguity because, in many cases, it reflects the way events are practically reported. During query processing, the missing intervals can be configured to be interpreted as null data or as continuation of the last reported state. Notice that the location specified in these records are relative to a reference (viz., the location of the superevent). Thus, the location value "near stage" is interpreted with respect

**Table 3.1:** Data instances of an evolving violent situation expressed in the E*ML model is presented as a table. The state variables are italicized in the "state" column. The "open_properties" column represents non-schema properties recorded for each instance.

| (violence subevent_of TroubleTownRally) | | | |
|---|---|---|---|
| occurs_during | occurs_at[ref=superevent] | state | open_properties |
| (14:32,14:34) | near stage | *agitation*:high | speaker_incitement:"speaker gives anti-government slogan" |
| | north-east corner | *agitation*:high | |
| | west-side | *agitation*:high | |
| | near temporary fence | *agitation*:escalating, *assault*: "physical fight with guards," *action*:{"people picking up stones," "people fleeing"} | |
| (14:34,14:37) | west-side | *action*:"people rushing west" | assault_target:"county office" |
| | north-east corner | *action*:"people rushing toward police vehicles" | comment:"police seem to start taking position"' |
| | near temporary fence | *action*:"people breaking fence," *assault*:"stone pelting toward police vehicles" | |
| (14:39,14:42) | near police vehicles | *retaliation*:"police taking positions with shields and guns" | |
| | north-east corner | *assault*:"stone and glass bottle pelting toward police vehicles," *retaliation*:"police surrounding perimeter" | |
| | south-side | *retaliation*:"police surrounding perimeter" | |
| | west-side | *action*:"crowd charging toward a govt. building," *assault*:"stone and glass bottle pelting at govt. building" | damage:"some windows are shattered" |
| (14:45,14:50) | near police vehicles | *assault*:"stone and glass bottle pelting at govt. building escalates," *action*:"new police force," *retaliation*:"tear gas being assembled" | damage:"external lights and all front windows broken" |
| | south-side | *assault*:"stone pelting," *retaliation*:"police firing in air," *injury*:"4 or 5" | comment:"the extent of injuries are not clear" |

to the polygon explicitly representing the meeting ground, or the polygon induced by finite-precision (latitude, longitude) value. In this example, `action`, `assault`, `injury`, etc. are state variables, while `comment` and `speaker_incitement` are open properties assigned to specific instances. As the example shows, an instance of a continuous event is partially structured like a tree, where the root node depicts the event instance, the second order nodes represent increasing time intervals, the third order nodes represent locations, the fourth order nodes represent "state" and "open property" elements, and the final level represents the properties themselves. In Table 3.1, all state and open properties are attributes. However, in general, these properties could also be relationships that link to other instance entities, thus making the structure only a partial tree.

**Function-based Properties.** We call a property of an entity `function-based` when the data type of the property is known, but the value of the property is computed by executing a function. This is a common functionality in many data models. In object-relational systems, methods are used to get values from functions. More recently, active XML systems generate new values by calling web services [Abiteboul et al., 2008]. In our setting, let us consider the use of experiential data (i.e., data captured through images and videos) in describing events. Let us consider a meeting event that has a property called `crowdedness`, which can have values from the set {`high, medium, low`}. We also assume this is a continuous event where `crowdedness` is a state variable that is updated every few minutes by calling a function $c(I)$ that computes on the live camera feeds $I$ from meeting. Thus, for any instance $i$, the function $c$ accepts $i$.`experienced_with` as input and after computing a rough density of human-like objects in the media, returns the value of `crowdedness` over time. In E*ML, functional properties are specified first by declaring the functions.

```
function getCrowdedness(set(image)) returns enum{high, medium, low}
```

The function is then used in the type definition.

```
open type monitoredMeeting::event(
crowdedness getCrowdedness(this.experienced_with.cameras[1,3,4][NOW-5,NOW])
)
```

where the argument of the function specifies the cameras to use and the time interval for which the images need to be sent to the function. As with many temporal systems, E*ML treats NOW as a special constant. In a fully sensor-based event monitoring scenario as found in pervasive computing applications [Hampapur et al., 2005], there might be many media processing functions each providing different "features" (functional values) of the event that can be state variables. In more complex situations, mostly in very controlled environments, functional properties can be object valued. For example, in a surveillance application, the participants of an activity can be automatically recognized, thus connecting the event to the `person` entity. So far, we have described the *subevent-of* as a user-asserted property. However, Gong and Jain [2007] have demonstrated that it is possible to compute video processing functions to instantiate the event-subevent structure of a composite event.

**Function-based Event Instantiation.** In addition to defining event properties, functions may also be used to generate event instances. The most familiar example is one of instantiating repeated events in a calendar, where the event class is defined, with a number of parameters like (*a*) whether the function is invoked at regular intervals or on demand (`invocation`), (*b*) if regularly invoked, how often is it invoked (`regularity`), (*c*) meeting periodicity (`periodicity`), (*d*) the dates of validity for the event class (`firstdate, lastdate`), and (*e*) whether the instantiated events are persistent or transient (i.e., whether the events are retained in the store after they are created), at the minimum. Let us consider the example of repeated events, and let us assume we are interested in an event type called `meeting` which is a subclass of the event `gathering` has the additional attributes `meetingRoom` and `ifPeriodic, firstDate, lastDate`. Thus,

```
open type meeting::gathering(
meetingRoom string;
invocation enum(regular, on_demand);
```

```
regularity enum(weekly, biweekly, monthly, quarterly, biannually, yearly);
periodicity enum(daily, weekly, monthly, quarterly, biannually, yearly);
firstDate dateTime;
lastDate dateTime;
isTransient boolean;

function instantiateMeeting(userDate) returns instance(meeting.meetingRoom);
)
```

The return statement of the instantiation function specifies that it returns an instance of the class `meeting` with the property `meetingRoom` filled in. To use this function, the user would create a partial instantiation of the event category as the following:

```
create prototype projectMeeting::meeting('E323', 'on_demand', 'biweekly',
'biweekly', '03/11/2010' '06/25/2012', 'false')
```

This declaration creates a template of how a meeting named `ProjectMeeting` will be created. When the user calls the instantiation function with a given date, the function returns `null` if the instance cannot be created on such a date; otherwise, it creates a temporary record of the meeting with all constants duly filled in from the prototype.

**Event Grouping.** The E*ML model supports the notion of named groups for events. A named group is a record having a declared name and a group definition. The structure of a group can be a set, a list or a graph. The member events of the group can be specified by assertions or by calling function. An event can belong to multiple groups, unless there is a unique membership constraint on the group. Groups can be nested, i.e., a group can be a member of another group. For example, in the declaration

```
function followEdge(event, edgeLabel) returns graph(event);

eventgroup evidenceTrail(
anchorEvent event;
trail followEdge(anchorEvent, causedBy);
)
```

the named group `evidenceTrail` uses the attribute `anchorEvent` to seed the event from which a graph will be constructed by transitively following all edges (i.e., property names) labeled `causedBy`. Event groups are used to implement collective events discussed in Section 2.3.6. We will discuss the construction of collective events after we define query constructs for the event model in the next chapter.

## 3.4.2 TOWARD A PHYSICAL MODEL FOR E* EVENTS

A physical model specifies how a logically defined data model can be stored on disk (and in memory) using a set of data structures. In this section, we discuss several different considerations that go into the design of an appropriate storage model for events defined through the E* model. However, we

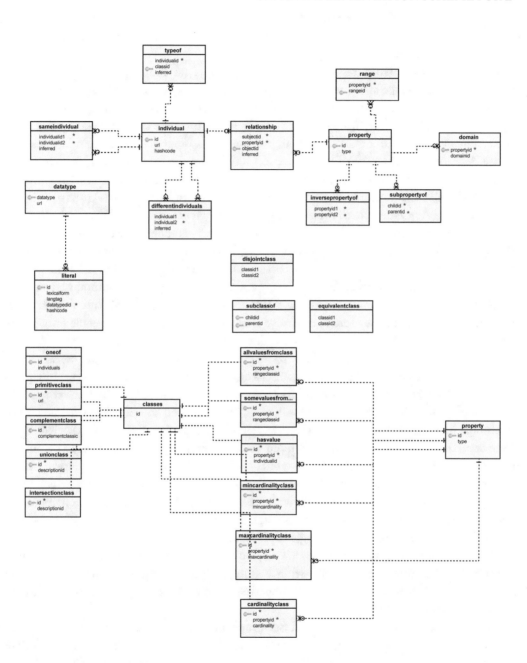

Figure 3.6: The Minerva schema.

will not prescribe a "best" storage model because it is an open research problem. Instead, we will illustrate how an event system can be developed based on a relational storage together with a number of auxiliary data structures.

**Storing Ontological Structures.** Since the E* model is an ontology, our first task is to present a relational storage structure for ontological graphs. Currently, several systems like Minerva [Heymans et al., 2008] and OntoMind [Al-Jadir et al., 2010] have been designed to store ontology classes and relationships (called *TBox* in ontology literature) as well as instances (called *ABox*). These systems take an RDF or OWL ontology document as input and store them in a relational database. As Al-Jadir et al. [2010], Theoharis et al. [2005] point out, storage strategies for ontologies can either be schema oblivious, schema aware or hybrid. In the schema oblivious strategy, there is essentially one table that captures all relationships in the form (`subject`, `predicate`, `object`) called a *triple store*. As a variant, each triple is assigned an explicit identifier, and the resulting structure is stored in a four-column table, called a *quad store*. This strategy is adopted by the Virtuoso semantic database[3] because having an identifier with each triple is required to implement reification (see Appendix A). The obvious advantage is that metadata and data can be processed in the same way. The drawback is poor efficiency. Performance can be improved by indexing each column, clustering on the predicate column, or creating materialized views [Hondjack et al., 2007]. All of these accelerators require extra storage cost, and they lead to expensive join queries. A common multi-table storage strategy has been adopted by Heymans et al. [2008]. They categorize tables of the database schema (see Fig. 3.6) into four types: atomic tables, TBox axiom tables, ABox fact tables and class constructor tables. The atomic tables include the following: `Ontology`, `PrimitiveClass`, `Property`, `Datatype`, `Individual` (for instances), `Literal` and `Resource`. The tables `SubClassOf`, `SubPropertyOf`, `Domain`, `Range`, `DisjointClass`, `InversePropertyOf` are used to keep TBox axioms. Other relationships like `rdf:type`, `rdf:comment`, etc., are also kept in separate tables. A view named `Relationship` is constructed as an entry point to object property triples and datatype property triples. An assertion like `humanEvent ⊑ event ⊓ ∃ participant.human` (a human event is an event in which some human participates) involves the `PrimitiveClass` table in which `human` and `event` are records, the `someValuesFrom` table containing the intermediate anonymous class `C1` that stands for `∃ participant.human`, and the `intersection` table containing the (`event`, `C1`) pair. The instances are stored in a single triple store.

Other multi-table storage strategies are also possible for ABox data in which each property is associated with a different table as shown in Figure 3.8. One can also use a multi-column table for the instances of each class such that all properties associated with this class become different columns as shown in Figure 3.7.

**Storing Instances of Inherited Types and Subproperties.** Let us separate the issues of storing declared properties and open properties of instances. Here we consider the storage of declared properties including inherited properties, thus making the problem nearly identical to the problem of physical design in an object relational database. There are several known techniques for implementing

---

[3] http://virtuoso.openlinksw.com/rdf-quad-store/

| Class 1 | | |
| --- | --- | --- |
| ID | Prop1 | Prop2 |
| id-1 | prop-1-val-1 | prop-2-val-1 |
| id-2 | prop-1-val-2 | prop-2-val-2 |

| Class 3 | | |
| --- | --- | --- |
| ID | Prop4 | Prop5 |
| id-5 | prop-4-val-1 | prop-5-val-1 |
| id-6 | prop-4-val-2 | prop-5-val-2 |

| Class 2 | |
| --- | --- |
| ID | Prop3 |
| id-3 | prop-3-val-1 |
| id-4 | prop-3-val-2 |

Figure 3.7: Multiple class tables each with different properties.

| Property 1 | |
| --- | --- |
| instance1-ID | value1 |
| instance2-ID | value2 |
| Property 2 | |
| instance3-ID | value3 |
| instance4-ID | value4 |

| Classes | |
| --- | --- |
| Class-1 | Instance-1-ID |
| Class-1 | Instance-2-ID |
| Class-2 | Instance-3-ID |
| Class-2 | Instance-4-ID |

Figure 3.8: Class Table and Individual Property Tables.

inheritance used by current object-relational databases. Commonly used techniques are one-table-per-hierarchy, one-table-per-type, and one-table-per-concrete-type. For us, the first approach will create one single table called event, and all declared properties of all its subclasses will be stored as attributes of this relation. For any instance of a logical subtype, non-applicable values are stored as null values. If one needs to recover instances that belong only to a subtype like meetingEvent, one can define an appropriate view to the properties that belong to that subtype with the native and the inherited properties. The advantage of this representation is that it is compact and avoids the cost of joins during query processing. However, one has to ensure that all integrity constraints we have discussed in the last chapter and this chapter have been reformulated to fit into this single-table schema. The second approach would create multiple tables, one for each declared open type; each subtype will be connected to its parent type through a join-key. While this is an intuitive design and achieves polymorphism really well, it is costly in terms of both updates and ad hoc queries that require a large number of joins. The third design also creates multiple tables, but only for the types that are concrete, i.e., the types that are more likely to be populated in instances. For example, there will be no table called events, but subtypes at the leaf-level of the event hierarchy will be stored as their own tables, and attributes of upper level tables will be incorporated into these tables.

Although the relational model does not have an explicit model for subproperties, it can be easily modeled within a relational framework because every subproperty can be modeled as a table with the additional integrity constraints. These constraints will limit the domain and range of the property to appropriate entities specified in the logical definition of the subproperty. Mapping properties to relations naturally allows one to add multiple parameters of a property by simply adding more attributes to the property tables.

**Storing Instances of Open Types and Relationships for Events.** An open type or an open relationship for events presents a number of challenges to the underlying storage system. Unlike a standard schema, an open type only declares a partial schema, and an instance can have an arbitrary number of additional properties, yet the system must support all standard data manipulation operations uniformly on the declared fragment and the undeclared fragment of the instances. Further, due to the inherent graph-like nature of the data, the storage strategy should facilitate graph-like operations over declared and undeclared fragments of instances. In terms of workloads, an event database is much less likely to be transactional or read-only; it is reasonable to assume that the data will be more insert-intensive.

A flexible storage option is to consider an *entity-partitioned triple store*, a model where the instances are stored in a set of triples stores so that each store corresponds to a declared entity type. In this model, conceptually, every instance of an entity type will be stored in its own triple store. Each triple store can be populated with both the declared as well as the undeclared fragments of an entity's properties. The entity classes are dictionary encoded. In one implementation, every class like `meeting_event` is represented by an integer (say 43). Every instance of the class has a system-wide unique identifier, like 43.239. Every data value having a discrete domain is also dictionary encoded. Since the instances have unique identifiers, an object pointer works like a "foreign key" from one triple store to another. Recently, there has been a number of studies exploring whether a triple-store should be implemented in a well-designed row-store (such as a relational system), a column store, or a bitmap-based system. We briefly review these options.

- *Using Row Stores.* A row store is a traditional database storage where sets of tuples are stored in data pages, clustered by one or more clustering attributes. Additional index structures are used to improve query performance. Triple stores have been implemented directly on database systems for a long time [MahmoudiNasab and Sakr, 2010]. Abadi et al. [2007] created a B-tree based implementation of a triple store using PostgreSQL. The system used three B+tree indices: one clustered on SPO (subject, property, object) and two un-clustered on POS (property, object, subject) and OSP (object, subject, property). Sidirourgos et al. [2008] has used its MonetDB/SQL module to use PSO (property, subject, object) as the clustering index. They point out that mature B+tree implementations support key-prefix compression, thus, in practice, not storing the entire property column.

- *Using Column Stores.* In contrast with row stores, column store [Stonebraker et al., 2005] is a storage scheme where the values in each column of a table are stored together. Column stores have been shown to provide greater efficiency in many applications such as data warehousing – since only a single column is stored at a time, the tuple header is eliminated; with a single type of value in every column, the data can be better compressed; for many queries only a few columns are retrieved and accessing only suitable columns reduce access cost for long tuples; novel query processing techniques [Idreos et al., 2009] can be applied to reduce the cost needed to create result tuples from affected columns during queries. Algorithms for performing physical level operations including scanning and column joining have been thoroughly investigated in column stores have been effectively used for geometric data types that support spatial operations – MonetDB/SQL[4] comes with an interface to the Simple Feature Specification of OpenGIS, which opens the route to develop GIS applications. The MonetDB/SQL/GIS module supports all objects and functions specified in the OGC "Simple Features for SQL" specification. Spatial objects are expressed in a text format and specified in the type and coordinates of spatial objects. Abadi et al. [2007] and Sidirourgos et al. [2008] have investigated the problem of storing RDF style data in column stores. Sidirourgos et al. [2008] has demonstrated how graph query patterns for SPARQL can be evaluated efficiently using column stores.

A head-to-head comparison shows no clear winner between a row store and a column store for triple style data. While one has the choice of partitioning each triple store with one table per property (i.e., like Fig. 3.8), not partitioning by property is often found to be a more scalable solution. Sidirourgos et al. [2008] has shown that with fewer data records a vertically-partitioned store has a better query performance; the non-partitioned row store demonstrates significantly better performance as the number of instances scales up.

- *Using Bitmap Indices.* The idea that a triple store can be viewed as different permutations of the three columns of a triple has been used in Hexastore [Weiss et al., 2008]. More recently, a number of groups have used the idea to create a bitmap index based implementation of permutations of the three columns of a triple store. McGlothlin and Khan [2008], for instance, create a dictionary of subjects and objects, and then constructs six tables: SOTable, POTable, PSTable, SSJoinTable, SOJoinTable and OOJoinTable. The first three tables have a similar structure. The PSTable, for example, creates a bit vector over all objects for each combination of property and subject. Thus, an entry in the PSTable would look like the following:

$$(3, 5, 0001100001)$$

which states that out of 10 objects encoded 0 . . . 9 in the database, objects 3, 4, 9 have a link from the subject encoded as 5 for property encoded as 3. The remaining three tables are join indices. The SSJoinTable encodes the SPARQL query

```
select ?p1, ?p2, bitvector(?s)
where (?s ?p1, ?o1), (?s, ?p2, ?o2)
```

---

[4]http://monetdb.cwi.nl/SQL/Documentation/SQL _002fGIS.html

thus creating a bit vector over all subjects over all pairs of properties that the subject participates in. Similarly, the SOJoinTable and the OOJoinTable encode the following queries, respectively.

```
select ?p1, ?p2, bitvector(?o1)
where (?s ?p1, ?o1), (?o1, ?p2, ?o2)

select ?p1, ?p2, bitvector(?o)
where (?s1 ?p1, ?o), (?s2, ?p2, ?o)
```

The positive aspect of a bitmap based representation is that bitmaps can be compressed easily using techniques like Fastbit [Wu et al., 2010], and they are amenable to parallelization. However, for storing events, bitmap based storage or indexing cannot be directly applied toward complex attribute domains such as spatial or temporal interval data.

The above discussion should show that there is no uniquely suitable storage strategy for event models, and the domain is open for new research. We conclude this section with a number of research considerations that must be considered in developing storage strategies for the E*ML model.

1. Since almost all event data and queries are likely to be indexed by time, it is useful to construct additional temporal indices for event instances.

   For row stores, this problem can be addressed by using many temporal indices that have been developed by the spatiotemporal data community. A fairly efficient temporal index is offered by RI-trees [Enderle et al., 2005]. The Relational Interval Tree (RI-tree) is a method to efficiently support intersection queries, i.e., reporting all intervals from the database that overlap (or touch or is equal to) a given query interval. It implements the classical interval tree [Cormen et al., 1990] using a relational database system. The structure of an RI-tree resembles a binary tree of height $h$, which covers the range $[1, 2^{h-1}]$ of potential interval bounds [Brochhaus et al., 2005]. It is called the virtual backbone of the RI-tree since it is not materialized, but only the root value $2^{h-1}$ is stored persistently in a metadata table. Traversals of the virtual backbone are performed by starting at the root value and proceeding in positive or negative steps i of decreasing length $2^{h-1}$, thus reaching any desired value of the data space in $O(h)$ CPU time and without causing any I/O operation. For the naive relational storage of intervals, the node values of the tree are used as artificial keys: Upon insertion of an interval, the first node that hits the interval when descending the tree from the root node down to the interval location is assigned to that interval. An instance of the RI-tree consists of two relational indexes. The indexes obey the relational schema lowerIndex(node, lower, id) and upperIndex(node, upper, id) and store the artificial key value node, the bounds lower and upper, respectively, and the id of each interval. Both of these indexes are defined by using the same relational schema. An interval is represented by a single entry in each of the two indexes, and therefore, $O(n/b)$ disk blocks of size $b$ suffice to store $n$ intervals. For inserting or deleting intervals, the node values are determined arithmetically, and updating the indexes requires $O(log_b n)$ I/O operations per interval.

For column stores, columns have their own identifiers, and column values are often sorted and indexed based on column positions. A temporal access structure like the interval-tree can be constructed as a secondary index such that the data pages of the tree point to (columnID, columnPosition) records. Since an RI-tree will require the use of a relational system, other non-relational choices may be more appropriate. For example, 1-dimensional R-trees are commonly found data structures that can perform similar functions.

On a similar note, event triples that are dependent on spatial or location should be additionally indexed, regardless of whether the data are stored in a row store or a column store.

2. Although our focus is on event-based information systems, many research issues that have been identified in mainstream information management research apply here, sometimes with a few additional considerations. We list a few such issues.

In the previous section, we have seen that while entity types exhibit single inheritance, entity instances can still be members of multiple user-defined categories because such classes may be defined through views, functions and group definitions. It is expected that event instances will be queried through these categories. For example, a user may query for instances of violent rallies that are also anti-Government rallies. It is reasonable to assume that each of the query terms "violent rally" as well as "anti-Government rally" are categories defined through nested views. Given these view definitions, a straightforward way to evaluate our query is to first unfold views to obtain member instances of each category and then perform an intersection. Let us assume an anti-Government rally is defined in the following manner.

```
aGRally(x) → rally(x), hasTargets(hasAgenda(x.leaderSpeech), z),
subClassOf+(z, Government)
rally(x) → gathering(x), hasCause(x, C), hasParticipants(x, P),
count(P) > 100
gathering(x) → event(x), hasParticipants(x, P), count(P) > 10
```

The following salient points related to index structures can be observed in these view definitions.

- Notice the use of the recursive predicate subClassOf+ that we have also used in entity declaration. Computing transitive closure for ontological relationships is a key operation in the E*ML data model. The problem of query evaluation over ontologies is beyond the scope of these lectures. However, it is easy to see that most transitive relationships in ontologies induce a directed acyclic graph over the concept nodes of an ontology graph. Several index structures have been proposed to efficiently compute reachability queries (i.e., queries that test if a path exists from one node in a DAG to another) over DAG-structured data (see [Yu and Cheng, 2010] for a survey). The goal of all these index structures is to avoid computing the full transitive closure by creating an index structure with which one can reconstruct the part of the transitive closure needed for a user query. Several of these structures have query time proportional to $log(n)$ where $n$ is the number of nodes, but index construction time is greater than $n^2$, and index size is $nk$ where $k$ is the number of disjoint paths in the graph; others have query time linear with $m$ where $m$ is the number of edges, but the index construction time and index size increase linearly with $m$. Most of these index structures do not consider graphs that have multiple edge labels – a characteristic of many ontologies. Exploration into indexing structure for multilabel graphs to facilitate multi-reachability queries (i.e., queries with multiple reachability tests) are still open for investigation.

• Information extracted from multimedia is a significant part of our framework. In the view above, suppose *hasAgenda* is a function which, given a single speaker audio input (like an interview of the rally leader) spots keyphrases that correspond to the agenda of the rally, and *hasTargets* is a function which, given a set of agenda-related phrases, matches them against dictionaries to find institutions or people the agenda negatively refers to. Prior work in multimedia information systems (e.g., [Chaudhuri et al., 2004]) have modeled media-related functions as "expensive predicates" and shown that for queries when only top-$k$ results must be returned, one can develop evaluation strategies that will search the minimum number of indices. Other techniques such as function caching, i.e., caching the results of expensive functions [Hellerstein and Stonebraker, 1993] for subsequent reuse, constructing new index structures for so called features (e.g., histograms [Gupta and Santini, 2000]), have been explored. Many of these techniques need additional index structures. However, indexing techniques and structures for efficient composition of arbitrary functions with different individual costs have not been investigated to date.

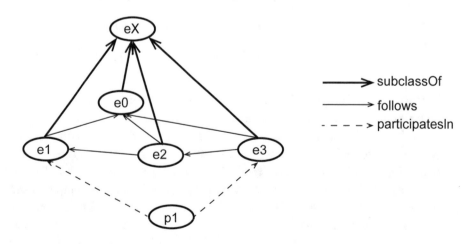

**Figure 3.9:** A graph query pattern.

3. As stated before, the instances of the E*ML model can be viewed as a large graph. We need to support graph queries where the query presents a graph pattern where the nodes represent subjects or objects and the edges represent properties or property paths. The task of the system is to find embeddings of the query pattern in the data graph. For example, the pattern at the end of Section 2.3.7 can be represented by the graph shown in Figure 3.9. A graph neighborhood based index structure called SPath has been proposed to facilitate graph pattern queries [Zhao and Han, 2010]. This index structure constructs a *neighborhood signature* for each node $u$ of the data graph. The signature consists of (a) a global lookup table, which, for each node label, returns a list of nodes having that label; (b) a histogram, which, up to a distance of $k$ from $u$, records the number of nodes of each label; and (c) and id-list, which records the actual ids of nodes counted in (b). The worst case cost for constructing the neighborhood index is $O(nm)$, while its space cost is $O(n + l + kln)$ where $l$ is the number of node labels; the cost of the id list, however, is $n^2$. With these structures in place, the query processing algorithm first decomposes the query pattern into a set of paths, which are then searched using the SPath index, and finally, the paths are instantiated from the data graph. The SPath algorithm does not directly consider graphs with edge-labels, although one can easily treat edge labels as a special kind of node.

The above discussions present the pragmatic and research issues related to implementing the E*ML data model. In the next chapter, we will consider the query language constructs and operators required for processing event information.

CHAPTER 4

# Querying Events

Specification and evaluation of event queries can be viewed from at least two different angles. The first is related to the detection of complex events from stored or streaming data. This aspect, briefly introduced in Sections 1.2.1 and 1.2.2, has a *detection semantics* [Adaikkalavan and Chakravarthy, 2006] and is not the focus of this lecture. The detection semantics has the setting that events occur in a stream, and the query monitors the stream to compute if a query is satisfied – hence, it places importance not only on the occurrence of events, but on when and how often the event can be detected. Instead, we consider querying a collection where events have been stored as first class data objects, together with associated information as described in the last two chapters. For the purposes of this chapter, we define an event query as a query on a collection of event-related information such that the query result returns event objects or the query conditions are applied to event objects. We do not present a full-length surface query language for events but, instead, present sketches of an event-centric query language, explore some intrinsic requirements of event-based queries, and describe the operations needed to meet these requirements. However, we will reuse fragments of the event expression sublanguage developed in the context of event detection systems. In the following, we assume that the reader is familiar with relational query processing [Garcia-Molina et al., 2002] and preferably XML query processing [Bruno et al., 2003, Chen et al., 2003, Jiang et al., 2003].

## 4.1 CHARACTERIZING EVENT QUERIES

We start by recapitulating a set of characteristic queries that an event-based information system must support, although many of the queries are not exclusively restricted to query event information only. For this discussion, we will use a syntax that inspired by the RDF query language SPARQL and the proposed social network query language SoQL [Ronen and Shmueli, 2009], suitably enhanced for our requirements.

*Q1.* **Spatiotemporal Queries.** "Which meetings are scheduled in this hotel today after the US representative's speech?" The query places conditions on locations that must be inside the hotel and must satisfy the temporal predicate *after* and restrict the results to *today*.

```
select m.id, m.name
where (m has_type meeting)
(m.occurs_at inside getLocation('Hotel Coronado')),
(m.date = today()),
      (m.occurs_in after
       (select s.occurs_in
```

```
            where (s has_type speech), (sp has_type person),
            (s speaker sp), (sp has_role[s]  'US Representative')
        )
    )
```

The query does not use a conventional `from` clause. Instead, it specifies the type of every query variable. For literal valued properties of an entity, one can use the standard (`attribute = value`) style, or a triple-style expression, whereas an entity reference is always represented in a triple style. The variable `sp` is existentially quantified, and the predicates `inside`, `after` are standard spatial and temporal predicates, interpreted over intervals and regions, respectively. The *has_role* predicate is parameterized by the speech (i.e., for this specific speech, the speaker has the role 'US Representative').

**Q2. Spatiotemporal Queries with Aggregates.** "Which political parties hold frequently meetings in the villages around my current location?" Here the query needs to compute an aggregate function to detect *temporal frequency*.

```
select p.name
where (m has_type meeting), (p has_type
political_party), (x has_type place),
        (m.organizer = p.name), (m.occurs_at inside x.boundaries()),
        (x instance_of 'village'), (distance(x.located_at,
myLocation()) < miles(10)),
        (temporal_count(m, year) > 8)
```

where `temporal_count` is an aggregate function that computes the number of occurrences of an event per unit time; x is an existentially quantified variable having the type 'place', and `boundaries()` is a function that returns the spatial geometry of a place. Notice that the aggregate function does not appear in the head of the query.

**Q3. Hierarchy-based Queries.** "Find subevents of the conference excluding the lunchtime and banquet-time events where a sponsor company is participating." This query uses the subevent hierarchy, as well as the hierarchy represented the categories and subcategories of sponsorship that the information system has explicitly modeled.

```
select e.name
where (c has_type conference), (n has_type company), (b has_type event)
        (e subevent_of+ c), (n subclass_of* c.sponsors),
                    not ((e subevent_of+ c.lunches)|
                        (e subevent_of+ (select b
                                            where (x has_type person),
                                                (x participates_in b),
                                                (x.works_for = n.name),
                                            )
                        )
                    )
```

The subquery shows a value-based join between x, a variable of the subquery and n, a variable of the outer query.

**Q4. Queries on Continuous Events.** "Find political meetings that became increasingly violent" needs to find a trend in the state variables associated with violence. To formulate this query, we need to specify a trend-computing aggregate function which accepts a temporally ordered list of values of a state variable over a time-interval, and returns, let us say, an enumerated value like increasing, decreasing or no change.

```
select m.name, m.date
where (m subclass_of+ 'political_meeting'),
(trend(m.agitation, m.occurs_in) = 'increasing' |
 trend(m.action, m.occurs_in) = 'increasing' |
 trend(m.assault, m.occurs_in) = 'increasing')
)
```

**Q5. Pattern Queries on the Event Graph.** "Find all occasions where a political leader made a comment and retracted it within 24 hours following protests inside and outside his/her own party." Here we are looking for all occurrences of the graph pattern including the event of the political leader making the comment, the reactions toward the comment, and the subsequent retraction event. We assume that a retraction event refers to an original statement and a retracted statement.

```
select ontological graph G
where (p has_type political_leader), (s1
has_type speech), (s2 has_type speech),
      (pa1 has_type political_party), (e1 has_type protest), (e2 has_type protest),
      (m1 has_type person), (m2 has_type person), (r has_type statement_retraction),
      (s1.speaker = s2.speaker), (s1.speaker.name = p.name), (s1 member_of pa1)
      (s1.occurs_during < s2.occurs_during - hours(24)),
      (e1 has_target s1), (m1 participates_in e1), (m1 member_of pa1),
      (e1.occurs_in after s1.occurs_in), (e1.occurs_in before s2.occurs_in),
      (e2 has_target s1), (m2 participates_in e1), not(m2 member_of pa1),
      (e2.occurs_in after s1.occurs_in), (e2.occurs_in before s2.occurs_in),
      (r.original_statement refers_to s1), (r.retracted_statement refers_to s2)
      (G graph_over (p, s1, s2, pa1, e1, e2, m1, m2, r))
```

The query conditions state that the protest events e1 coming from members of the speaker p's political party pa and e2 coming from a nonmember of the party, targeted the speech s, and the retracted speech came less than 24 hours after the original speech. The expression ontological graph at the head of the query specifies that the nodes included in the last predicate must be ontologically correct, and include all mandated properties for each entity type returned. Thus, the result of the query is a set of graphs, each of which is an induced subgraph graph over the list of nodes bound to the query variables, augmented to include additional properties needed by the ontology.

***Q6.*** **Neighborhood Queries on the Event Graph.** "What happened following the argument that started during the US representative's speech?" Let us assume that the "argument" event is a graph pattern representing multiple people expressing opinions and counter-opinions over a certain topic or remark, for longer than 10 minutes. Let us first represent a view to capture this phenomenon.

```
create view argument(original_s, original_o) as (
  select ontological graph G
  where (orginal_s has_type speech), (original_o has_type opinion),
        (s has_type speech), (o has_type opinion),
        (G graph_over ((original_s expresses original_o), (s expresses o),
                   (o (accepts|rejects)^k, (k > 4)) original_o)),
        (G.duration > minutes(10)).
)
```

In this view definition, `original_s`, `original_o` are parameters passed on to the view. Notice that the regular edge expression `(accepts|rejects)^ k, (k > 4)` (see also [Alkhateeb et al., 2009, Pérez et al., 2008]) follows the transitive chain of accepting and opposing opinions that starts from the original opinion, asserting that the length of the chain must exceed 4. In contrast to the previous example, the specification of G includes the edges `expresses, accepts` and `rejects`. The `duration` property of the graph G is computed from the time intervals of all events under G. The query does not explicitly represent the speakers whose speeches are associated with the opinion because they are included as a mandatory property of the `speech` object. The size of the graph is determined by the size of the transitively generated DAG over opinions. Next, we interpret the query "what happened after ..." as a graph of events that are "related to" (i.e., has any event-to-event or event-to-media edge), and occurring after the argument event. A potential difficulty in posing this query is that we have to determine how to define the conditions that would terminate the recursive navigation outward from the argument event through the chain of related events. If no such stopping condition is satisfied, the query may potentially be unbounded.

```
select ontological graph G include media
using argument
where (s has_type speech), (op1 has_type opinion), (e has_type event),
      (sp has_type person), (l has_type edge_label),
      (s.date = today()), (s.speaker has_role 'US Representative'),
      (s expresses op1),
      (G graph_over (event_nodes(argument(s, op1)) l* e)),
      maxNodes(G) = 100
```

where the function `event_nodes` extracts the event nodes from the result of the view arguments, `edge_label` is the property of all edge labels, and `l*` recursively traverses over all event-to-event edges. The constraint on the total nodes of the graph limits the recursive expansion of the query.

*Q7.* **Event Association Queries.** "How are the litigation events filed by the opposition against the Government in the last 6 months related to the corruption debates that occurred last May?" This represents a class of queries where a query *seeks a path or subgraph (with edge-label filters)* that forms a reachability network, among a set of nodes in the event graph.

```
select ontological graph G
where (l has_type litigation), (pa has_type party), (p has_type person)
      (l.defendant ='Government'),
      (l.plaintiff = set(p)), (p member_of pa), (pa has_role 'Opposition'),
      (l.date < now()), (l.date >= now()-months(6)),
      (d has_type debate), (d has_topic 'corruption'), (d has_target 'Government),
      (d.occurs_in daterange(05/01/2010, 05/31/2010)),
      (G1 graph_over (l, p, pa)), (G2 graph_over (d, ($x subevent_of d))),
      (G connect_by_graph(G1, G2,
                          include_edge_label('subevent_of', 'causes',
                                             'evidence_of')))
```

The `connect_by_graph` clause computes multi-reachability between the nodes of G1 and G2, and G returns G1, G2 as well as their connecting graph.

*Q8.* **Event Composition Query.** The graph queries above represent a form of composition because it constructs a new graph-structured entity by putting together selected items from the event database. A different flavor of event composition, more in tune with the complex event processing community is represented by the query "Create a new event called 'public life disruption' by accumulating political meetings in the city of Patna occurring on 7 consecutive days followed by traffic jams longer than at least one hour after the end of the meetings. To this event collection, add two images of the traffic jam from the first and the last meetings." Let us assume that traffic jam is a Boolean variable reported every 5 minutes by a news service for different streets of the city. This can be written:

```
select event graph 'public life disruption' as PLD
   where
   (PLD occurs_somewhere_at city('Patna')), (PLD includes X, I),
   (X has_type sequence(p)), (I has_type image),
   (p has_type 'political meeting'), (X duration days(7)),
   (p.next().occurs_in = p.occurs_in + days(1)),
   (j has_type sequence('traffic jam')), (j.duration >= hours(1)),
   (j meets X), (j.occurs_at near p.occurs_at),
   (I includes random(j[1].images,2), random(j[7].images,2))
```

The query illustrates how sequences are treated in the system. It constructs a named graph which is ontologically consistent with an event containing a 7-day sequence of political meetings such that the time gap between one meeting and the next is 1 day; further, there is at least an hour-long traffic jam event (sequence) such that every occurrence of the jam event

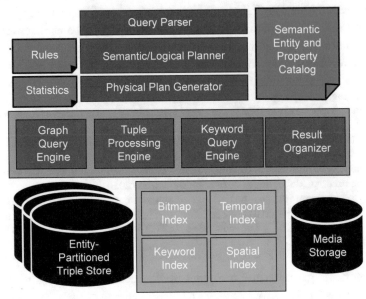

**Figure 4.1:** The general processing architecture of an event query processor. It loosely assumes the entity-partitioned triple store model described in Chapter 3.4. The Media Store contains the media information, and the media feature store contains the properties extracted or computed from the media. We assume the media feature store to be relational, with special functions for feature comparison.

is spatially near that of the political party's meeting. The predicate `meets` is borrowed from Allen's interval algebra [Allen and Ferguson, 1994]. Also note that the `duration` property of an event sequence is the sum of the durations of its constituent events, and the assignment of PLD's location to the `Patna` city restricts the spatial scope of `p` and `j` to the same city. The image set `I` are included in the new event PLD by first selecting traffic jam events related to the first and last days of the selected meeting sequence, and then selecting two random images from the image set associated with these jam events. Since no edge construction predicates are stated, the edges of the PLD graph preserve the edges found in the data.

## 4.2   A QUERY PROCESSING ARCHITECTURE

The architecture of a conventional query processing system [Garcia-Molina et al., 2002] consists of (a) a query parser that transforms a user's query into an algebraic expression and applies algebraic rewriting rules, (b) a logical planner that transforms the algebraic expression into a plan tree of operators, (c) a physical plan generator that select the appropriate *execution primitives* (e.g., which indices to use) and the data passing plan between these operators, and (d) an evaluation engine that executes the physical plan. The architecture uses several auxiliary pieces of information along the way. A catalog is consulted to use the knowledge of the schema in step (a); sometimes a set of rules are used to perform the algebraic rewriting in step (b); statistics like relations sizes and attribute value distributions are used to estimate selectivity and cost of query processing in steps (b) and (c). An event query processing architecture (Figure 4.1) adapts and extends these components to cater to the special semantics that events carry, and the heterogeneity of query types presented in the last section.

To illustrate the components of Figure 4.1, we walk through the query processing steps of *Q1*. Let us assume we have three stores for meeting(M), speech(S) and speaker(K), and that speaker store has a parameterized relationship with a single parameter. An initial plan corresponding to *Q1* can be as follows:

$$\pi_{\texttt{m.id,m.name}}(\sigma_{\texttt{m.date=today()}}(\bowtie_{\theta_1} (\texttt{getLocation('Hotel Coronado')}, \bowtie_{\theta_2} (\texttt{M}, \pi_{\$I}(\bowtie_{\theta_3}^G (\texttt{S,SP}))))))$$

where
$\theta_1 = \texttt{inside(m.occurs\_at, location)}$
$\theta_2 = \texttt{after(m.occurs\_in, \$I)}$
$\bowtie^G$ is a graph join with condition

$\theta_3 = \texttt{S[(id speaker K.id),(id occurs\_in \$I)], K[(id has\_role[S.id] 'US Representative')]}$

The graph join operation is motivated by join operations in RDF stores, but it is "customized" to take into account the entity stores that come into play. In this example, the first condition is a so called star-join (because the subject of the triple is the joining column), and an inter-store join uses two joining parameters – the ids of the speaker and the speech. We will describe the impact of the edge parameterization in Section 4.4.

To generate this initial plan, the query translator must consult the catalog to utilize the schema information for evaluating the query. Although the query uses a condition (speaker has_type person), the entity speaker materializes the properties of person, and hence this condition can be dropped. The initial plan generation process itself uses a set of rules – the join conditions between S and K have been left as graph joins, but those with M have not because the $\theta$-joining conditions involve temporal and spatial predicates.

Step 2 of the plan involves algebraic and semantic rewriting of the initial plan to improve efficiency. The most obvious rule, used in relational systems is to push selections down, which, in this case, means applying the selection predicate (date = today) on M. Many of these rules are standard, and we do not discuss them here. More important cases, however, are semantic rules associated with events. For example, it is known that event instances mostly specify their time and location of occurrence. Since the desired meeting is today, and it is after the US Representative's speech, the speech must occur either today or immediately prior to today's date. This semantic constraint adds a temporal condition that can be stated: (s occurs_in today()) XOR (s occurs_in nearest(today())). It is important to observe the order of these XOR-ed two predicates. If the first predicate is satisfied, the second is not evaluated. A different semantic optimization can be performed on the location of the meeting. If the getLocation function (which will produce a single value) can be evaluated earlier, it can be passed down the query, thus eliminating the need for the first $\theta$-join. This is similar in spirit to the query evaluation technique of *sideways information passing* [Beeri and Ramakrishnan, 1987] in Datalog. However, in our case, we inspect all conditions specifically to identify if the temporal and locational bounds for all events can be indirectly obtained without changing the semantics of the query. This would transform the first plan into the following:

$$\pi_{\text{m.id,m.name}}(\bowtie_{\theta_2} (\sigma_{\text{m.date=today()},\text{inside(m.occurs\_at,getLocation('Hotel Coronado'))}}$$

$$\text{M}, \pi_{\$I}(\bowtie^G_{\theta_4} (\text{S},\text{SP}))))$$

where
$\theta_4$=S[(id speaker K.id),(id occurs_in \$I), (\$I=today() XOR (\$I nearest today()))], K[(id has_role(S.id) 'US Representative')]

Step 3 of the query planning process uses the different query processors and index structures, and how data are passed between them. We only illustrate the salient aspects of the physical query plan.

1. An unusual part of this architecture is the set of multiple processors. In a standard query engine that allows multiple types of data, it is customary to have a large collection of operators, each with its own signature but a central planner and execution controller that orchestrates how data flows through the correct set of operators for a specific query. A processor can be thought of as a set of operators with its own execution control logic, which, given a subplan, uses its own logic to produce a physical plan for that subplan. Note however, that all data is available to all processors. Thus, while an entity partitioned triple store is designed with the graph nature of the data in mind, the tuple processing engine can treat it as basic relational store. Similarly, a processor can use any indices that it needs. A B-tree index can be used for both the graph processor and the tuple processor.

2. In this architecture, the plan is partitionable – the $\theta_4$ joining portion can be executed by the graph engine; the outer part of the plan (i.e., everything from $\theta_2$-join and after) can be handled by the tuple processor; the selection operation over M can be executed by either the tuple processor or the graph processor, but using the tuple processor allows these subplans to be executed concurrently.

3. The graph processing component can use the temporal index for computing the overlap between the today() interval and the occurrence intervals over all speeches. If the second predicate of the XOR operation has to be computed, the nearest function can be computed by breaking up the timeline into disjoint segments and performing a join with the occurrence intervals of the speeches. As an alternate subplan, the occurrence intervals could be sorted by

starting time, and the closest speech can be found directly. The plan can be further optimized by using the selectivity of the 4-tuples of K that have the relatively rate constant 'US Representative'. The choice among these two plan options is made by estimating their selectivity using the statistics module.

4. The star-join pattern is characteristic of RDF Join algorithms and can be evaluated efficiently using bitmap indices [McGlothlin and Khan, 2008].

5. The graph engine represents graphs as edge-sets, i.e., as a relation over triples. Therefore, passing the triples from a graph processor to a tuple processor is a straight forward data movement operation. In fact, all the processors construct tuple packets to transfer data between them.

6. We have assumed, for simplicity, that the `getLocation` function call is like an external bounding box service that returns the covering latitude and longitude pairs for a named location, and the location of the meetings to be point entities. This the *inside* predicate can be quickly evaluated with an R-tree style spatial index. For a more elaborate setting, more complex methods can be used for point-in-polygon tests.

## 4.3   THE SEMANTIC CATALOG

We saw in the last section that the query processor uses the catalog for several purposes, including the formulation of the initial query plan and the subsequent query reformulation for optimization. The catalog is a collection of materialized data structures that carry schema information. For instance, it maintains a number of mappings between the conceptual model and the physical model, and it is internally queried by the planning modules for store selection and predicate ordering. We illustrate this using *Q2*. The user query specifies 3 entity types – `meeting`, `political_party` and `place`. Let us assume the query is valid because these entities are described in the E*ML conceptual schema of the application. However, the physical stores corresponding to these entities are unknown to the user. The catalog maps the declared entities and properties to physical stores. Let us say the physical model has four stores called `personalMeeting`, `socialMeeting`, `politicalMeeting` and `businessMeeting` and the concept `Meeting` maps to each of them. To formulate the query, the translator has to collect all conditions related to the variable m and determine that it has a property `organizer` whose value is joined to an attribute of the `politicalParties`. This amounts to a catalog lookup for a store that is mapped to the entity `meeting` having has a property called `organizer`, and it has a connection to the `politicalParties` store," leading to the result `politicalMeeting`. However, if the result of the lookup is non-unique, the rest of the user query will be sent to all stores matching the lookup results. A similar issue occurs for variable x, which is known to be of type `place`, is an instance of `village` and must satisfy two spatial predicates. The catalog also uses an index of property names and occurrence counts for all stores, as well as all property values that are strings. To select the store for x, the catalog function looks for a store name `village` having a property called `located_at` or a properties named `village` within a store named `place`. This, of course, can be problematic. Consider two different store schemas: placeid, place_type, place_name, location where `place_type` can have the value "village" and *villagesid*, village, location where the column name specifies the data record to be about villages. In these cases, the mapping between the store schema and the E\*ML model must be specified more precisely. In the first case, mappingentity(village) member_of domain(place.place_type) states that the E\*ML entity called village can be found among the domain (i.e., value set) of column `place_type` of the store `place`. In the second case, `mapping(entity(village) equivalent_to villages)`, stating that each record of store `villages` is an instance of the E\*ML entity `village`. The complete specification of the mapping language is beyond the scope of this book. The interested reader is referred to Gupta et al. [2010]. However, the initial plan generation algorithm must use these mappings to produce the correct plan.

## 4.4   AN ALGEBRAIC FRAMEWORK FOR E\*ML QUERY PROCESSING

In Section 3.4.1, we stated that the E\*ML type system uses a number of basic scalar types, geometric types and media types as well as the constructor types of eumeration, set, list, time-series, tuple, union and graph, which is further specialized into general graphs, directed acyclic graphs and trees. The example queries have shown the use of several of these types and constructors. The operations for most of these data types are well known and are not described in further detail.

Most event applications will operate at a level higher than the basic data manipulation level and, therefore, will need to combine these operations into more complex algebraic constructs that can be directly used in performing event-level manipulations of data. For example, an application that performs spatiotemporal analysis of events will need spatiotemporal groupings of events that satisfy a selection condition. In this case, the spatiotemporal grouping will need to combine multiple lower-level operators to perform the operation efficiently. We present a brief account of the basic data manipulation operations and some examples of higher level operations.

**Basic data manipulation.** As we saw in Section 4.1, the primary result object of a query is a set of tuple of heterogeneous data types. When a set of graphs is produced as a response to a query (e.g., in *Q5*), the arity of the result tuple is 1. Therefore, the tuple processor is the "primary" engine for queries, and it performs standard tuple-set operations including

(a) tuple construction ([.]),

(b) projection on attributes ($\pi(t, A)$) where $t$ is a tuple and $A$ is a set of projected attributes,

(c) projection on attributes with renaming ($\pi_r(t, (A, N))$), where $A$ are projected attributes and $N$ are new names,

(d) tuple concatenation ($\circ(t_1, t_2)$), which tuple $t_1$ is extended with the content of tuple $t_2$,

(e) generalized projection ($\pi_f(t, f(.), N)$ where a function $f$ is on an input tuple $t$ is computed, and the output tuple contains a new attribute $N$ corresponding to the result of the function,

(f) selection ($\sigma_\phi(T)$) where $T$ is a set of tuples and $\phi$ is a selection predicate,

(g) join ($\bowtie_\theta (T_1, T_2)$), where $T_1$, $T_2$ are tuple sets and $\theta$ is a joining predicate; a null-predicate results in a Cartesian Product,

(h) antijoin ($\rhd(T_1, T_2, A_1, A_2)$), where $A_1$, $A_2$ are attributes to satisfy the antijoin condition,

(i) leftouterjoin ($\ltimes(T_1, T_2, A_1, A_2)$),

(j) grouping ($\gamma(T, A, [p])$), where the tuple-set $T$ is grouped by the values of attributes $A$, and $p$ is a set of optional parameters. If $A$ is a spatial or temporal attribute, this grouping parameter may specify the granularity at which the grouping occurs. For example, in an event-based spatial analytics application [Singh et al., 2010], a grouping operation may use location as the grouping variable with grid origin and grid size as parameters.

(k) sorting ($S(T, A, p)$) where $p$ is the sorting parameter for ascending or descending sort.

These operators are standard in most query processors, but due to the heterogeneity of data types in attributes, the tuple processor does not look "inside" the data unless it is a "known" data type. All other data are pushed to other operators or delegated to other processors.

**Graph Manipulation.** The graph manipulation framework is a little more complex. Using our example in Section 4.2, let us consider the plan fragment $\pi_{\$I}(\bowtie^G_{\theta_3} (\text{S,SP}))$ where

$\theta_3 = \pi_{\$I}(\text{S}[(\text{id speaker K.id}),(\text{id occurs\_in \$I})],$
$\text{K}[(\text{id has\_role[S.id]} \ '\text{US Representative'})])$

The subplanner within the graph processor will first rewrite this query by separating out the edge parameter. The internal model of a parameterized edge partitions a triple store into a "regular triple set" and an "edge property triple set." The regular triple set has a `tripleID` column that serves the edge identifier column and serves as the subject column of the edge property triple set. The $\theta_3$ part can then be rewritten as the following:

$\pi_{\$I}((\text{S.id S.speaker K.id}), (\text{S.id occurs\_in \$I}),$
$\text{e:}(\text{K.id has\_role} \ '\text{US Representative'}), (\text{e speaker S.id}))$

where e is a tripleID/subject. Also note that the predicate has been "normalized" by moving the store identifiers into the variables. Next, let us consider the time interval \$I. The time interval is not stored within the triple store but is replaced by a surrogate identifier that points to a separate `TimeInterval` data object. Thus, the query is transformed to the following:

$\pi_{\text{getInterval(TI(id))}}((\text{S.id S.speaker K.id}), (\text{S.id occurs\_in TI(id)}),$
$\text{e:}(\text{K.id has\_role} \ '\text{US Representative'}), (\text{e speaker S.id}))$

Next, the plan separates out the edge property condition to produce the plan fragment:

```
project getInterval(TI(id)) (
```

```
    apply (join ((
            project S.id, TI(id), edgeID(K.id
has_role 'US Representative') as e(
              gproject( (S.id S.speaker K.id), (S.id occurs_in TI(id)),
                        (K.id has_role
'US Representative') [Speaker S, Speech K]
              )
            ), EdgeProp(e speaker S.id)
        ))
    )
)
```

The innermost `gproject` clause is a pattern evaluation function evaluated by the graph engine using its indices on the stores `Speaker` and `Speech`, and the result of the evaluation is a set of 3-edge graphs, each of which satisfies the pattern. Each connected graph is converted to a tuple set (along with the `tripleIDs`) and sent to the tuple processor. The `apply` function performs the join operation between this result and the `EdgeProp` table (i.e., the edge property triples table). Finally, the outermost generalized projection operation produces the actual time interval that is passed on to the upper levels of the query as shown before. `gproject` is one of several graph functions used by the graph engine. We list several other single-graph operations in Table 4.1 and explain their meanings. Other graph-theoretic operations like `indgree`, `outdegree`, `degree-distribution`, `shortest-path`$(n_1, n_2)$, `edge-disjoint paths`$(n_1, n_2)$, `centrality`$(f)$ where $f$ is a centrality function are not included in the table. In addition, there are binary operations on graph-pairs including

(a) `merge` $(\oplus(g_1, g_2))$ to perform an edge and node union of graphs $g_1$, $g_2$, if no common nodes are found, the graphs are disjoint, and cannot be merged according to the E*ML principles.

(b) `difference`$(\ominus(g_1, g_2, p))$ uses the parameter p to compute node set difference or edge set difference between $g_1$ and $g_2$.

(c) `connect`$(\otimes(g_1, g_2, E))$ to connect two graphs with the edge set $E$.

The physical plan for operations like `gproject` uses bitmap operations. Table 4.2 specifies operations on the bitmap indices. To see how these operations work, consider the fragment:

```
gproject((S.id S.speaker K.id), (S.id occurs_in TI(id))),
         (K.id has_role 'US Representative')[Speaker S, Speech K])
```

An unoptimized plan for this fragment can be given:

```
K_bitmap = POSelect('has_role', 'US Representative');
convert K_bitmap to K_set;

for each K in K_set
```

| Table 4.1: Operations for manipulating single graphs (adapted from Gupta et al. [2010]). | |
|---|---|
| `emptygraph(G)` | creates empty graph named G |
| `rename(g,G)` | renames a graph object as G |
| `roots(g)` | returns nodes with no incoming edges |
| `leaves(g)` | returns nodes with no outgoing edges |
| `scangraph(p,g)` | performs a scan operation over the edges that are evaluated to satisfy predicate p |
| `selectNodeLabels(p,g)` | selects a set of node labels satisfying predicate p |
| `selectNodes(p,g)` | selects a subset of nodes based on predicate p |
| `selectEdges(p,g)` | selects a subset of edges based on predicate p |
| `gproject(pat,g)` | projects a set of subgraphs that satisfies a graph pattern **pat** using a DAG index [Chen et al., 2005] when the graph is a DAG and a bitmap or a profile index [He and Singh, 2008] when it is not |
| `label(g)` | accepts a graph g and returns a copy of it by replacing the node-ids by node labels, and edge-ids by edge-labels |
| `flattenPropTree(pLabel),P` | accepts a property label **pLabel** from property tree P and returns a set of subproperties of label **pLabel** |
| `induce(N,g)` | given a node set N in graph g, returns the subgraph induced by N |
| `reachable(n1,n2,ei,g)` | whether node n2 is reachable n1 by traversing edges satisfying regular expression ei |
| `getTransitiveAncestors(n,Label,k,g)` | get k levels of ancestors of node n, by following the transitive edge label **Label** |
| `getTransitiveDescendants(n,Label,k,g)` | get k levels of descendants of node n, by following the transitive edge label **Label** |
| `neighbors(N,k,ei,ex,g)` | given nodes N, returns the k-neighborhoods of each node in N, such that the edges satisfy the regular expression ei, and do not satisfy the regular expression ex. |
| `LCA(N, Label,g)` | find the least common ancestor of node set N by traversing the transitive edge label **Label** |
| `dagPath(n1, n2, Label,D)` | find the paths connecting nodes n1 to n2 along transitive edge label **Label** for DAG D |
| `nodePath(n1, n2, ei,ex,g)` | find the paths connecting nodes n1 to n2 edges, satisfy the regular expression ei, and do not satisfy the regular expression ex |
| `centerpiece(N,g)` | given a node set N, compute the centerpiece subgraph intervening the nodes in N [Tong and Faloutsos, 2006] |
| `unfoldPropertyChain(chID)` | compute and materialize derived edges by unfolding property chains identified by property chain ID **chID**. Property chains are specified by a positive, non-recursive first order rule |

| Table 4.2: Bitmap operations referred to in Section 3.4.2 and adapted from McGlothlin and Khan [2008]. | |
|---|---|
| `POTable(pid default null, oid default null)` | nodeBitIdx for subjects |
| `PSTable(pid default null, sid default null)` | nodeBitIdx for objects |
| `SOTable(sid default null, oid default null)` | propBitIdx for properties |
| `bitAND(nodeBitIdx, nodeBitIdx)` | produces nodeBitIdx |
| `bitAND(propBitIdx, propBitIdx)` | produces propBitIdx |
| `SSJoin(pid1, pid2)` | produces nodeBitIdx for subjects |
| `SOJoin(pid1, pid2)` | produces nodeBitIdx for subjects |
| `OOJoin(pid1, pid2)` | produces nodeBitIdx for objects |
| `bitOR(nodeBitIdx, nodeBitIdx)` | produces nodeBitIdx |
| `bitOR (propBitIdx, propBitIdx)` | produces propBitIdx |
| `idx2nids(nodeBitIdx)` | set of nodeIDs whose bit is 1 in nodeBitIdx (project nodes) |
| `idx2pids(propBitIdx)` | set of propIDs |
| `POSelect(objNodeBitIdx, pid default null)` | nodeBitIdx for subjects. objNodeBitIdx tells us the bound object nodes. With a pid, we can get the binding of subject nodes which satisfies (sub pid boundObjId) |
| `SPSelect(subNodeBitIdx, pid default null)` | nodeBitIdx for objects |
| `SOSelect(subNodeBitIdx, objNodeBitIdx)` | propBitIdx for properties |
| `select(edgeSet, filters)` | returns edgeSet that satisfy the filters |
| `memoize(edgeSet)` | keeps a set of edges, typically returned from other operations into the memory, and returns a handle to it for future use |

```
    S_bitmap = POSelect('S.speaker', K);
    put (K, S_bitmap) in temp1 collection;
end;

for each (K, S_bitmap) in temp1
  convert S_bitmap to S_set;
  for each S in S_set
    TI(id) = PSSelect(S, 'occurs_in');
    put (K, S, TI(id)) in result collection;
  end;
end;

output result;
```

**Higher Level Operations.** Beyond the fine grained operations we have discussed so far, an event information system must consider higher level operations that are closer to application needs. Many of these operations can be built by constructing algorithms on top of these base operations, and potentially by constructing new operators that combine the functionality of some base operators. The following are examples of higher level operations that should be supported by an event information system.

- *Recursive Union over Event Hierarchies.* A recursive union operation creates a set (or bag) at some node of a hierarchy created by the `subevent-of` relationship and recursively populates the set by collecting appropriate data at each level of the hierarchy. An operation that.gathers all media objects of all subevents of an event performs a recursive union. In some cases, the hierarchies need not be traversed explicitly. To create a timeline for all meetings in a metropolitan area, one must collect (`meetingID`, `name`, `time`, `location`) tuples over the subclass hierarchy of meetings. However, this computation can avoid recursion if all meeting objects have an auxiliary index like Dewey encoding of a tree, such that the recursive union amounts to prefix computation.

- *Event Similarity.* Similarity between two data objects is usually measured by computing a similarity (or distance) metric in a high dimensional property space. Similarity measures for structured data objects assume that all objects have a number of common descriptors, and a similarity measure can be described for each; an overall similarity score can be computed by computing an aggregate function like weighted average on the individual property similarity scores. For events, one could thus compute similarity by considering the temporal distance , spatial distance modulo a granularity, media-feature similarity, as well as thematic similarity based on semantic distances on keywords. However, event similarities can also be computed based on occurrence patterns [Obweger et al., 2010, Suntinger, 2009], including event frequencies.

- *Event Relatedness.* A common operation in many event-based application is to find "events related to this event." While event similarity finds events based on a notion of "closeness" defined as a function of event properties, event relatedness is based on graph proximity. A relatedness finding algorithm performs a neighborhood search to find top-$k$ connected event nodes that satisfy user-specified conditions including (i) whether subevents should be included, (ii) if nodes with deeper subevent descendants will have higher weights, (iii) weights associated with each labels, (iv) weight formulae associated with the length of edge chains (e.g., weights diminish by a fraction with more distant elements), and (v) weights based on some centrality measure of nodes (e.g., pagerank [Brin and Page, 1998]).

We conclude this chapter by giving an example of a new operator that facilitates higher level event operations. A common pattern in several applications is to construct a result graph by first identifying a set of nodes that belong to the graph and then computing the subgraph induced by these nodes, followed by augmenting this "seed" graph by adding more edges that satisfy some query conditions. Very often, we have a situation where there are $k$ different node sets whose induced subgraphs need to be merged to produce the result graph. However, if $N_1$, $N_2$ are node sets then the operation $merge(\texttt{induced}(N_1), \texttt{induced}(N_2))$, it will not contain the edges between a node from $N_1$ and another from $N_2$; more operations are required to get all edges amongst these nodes. Since the operation is very common, we create a new operator `union-merge` $\biguplus(N_1, N_2) = \texttt{induced}(N_1 \cup N_2)$, where $\cup$ is the set union operation.

# CHAPTER 5

# Storytelling with Events

Modeling event-based information systems enables one to create several next generation applications. One such application is *storytelling*. There has been significant prior work in how computers can be used to assist the creation of stories. Much of this research is directed toward the presentation of multimedia stories based on user feedback [Brooks, 1996], or toward interactive story telling, where the system needs to interact with the user who can change the course of the story at bifurcation points, and the system has to adjust itself to keep the narrative flowing [Cavazza et al., 2009, Riedl and Stern, 2006]. In contrast with these efforts, a story, in our case, is a conveying of events, using appropriately arranged event descriptors, together with media elements like pictures or videos. Let us consider a scenario in which someone keeps a chronicle of his/her daily life – places he/she visits, people he/she meets, family gatherings, and so on. Each time he/she experiences an interesting or possibly memorable event, he/she takes pictures or videos, and adorns them with declared or open properties from the E*ML language to create event instances to which these media objects are witnesses. After a year of collecting events, he/she wants to create "stories" that would contain events and event descriptors, media and his/her own add-on narrations; the stories would be created for different people in his/her social circuit. To facilitate this process, he/she would like to use a software system that constructs an event database using his/her events and event-annotated media; at the time of storytelling, he/she would pick his/her audience and some general conditions for the story he/she would like to compose, and have the system produce a set of connected event clusters, together with media, that might provide the raw material for his/her storytelling needs. Informally, a request could be "a story for my mother about people I met last year," or "a story for my journalist friend Joseph about interesting personalities I met during my last two trips abroad." In this section, we will formally describe the storytelling problem as an event mining task, present a more formal story request language and an algorithmic approach to solve the mining problem. Throughout this process, we show that storytelling is not a completely algorithmic process, but is a human process facilitated by event mining techniques.

## 5.1 FORMULATING THE PROBLEM

Let $G = \{V, E, L\}$ be a connected event graph where $V$ is the set of nodes, $E$ is the set of edges and $L$ is the set of edge labels; let us assume at least edge labels `subclass-of`, `subevent-of`, `follows`, `participates-in`, `located-in` and `occurs-during` have been populated in $G$ and have the semantics discussed in previous chapters. Let us also assume that event participants in $G$ are connected in a social network $S_N$ of a user, and that $O(G)$ is an ontology that is used to define the events in $G$. A **story request** $Q$ specifies a set of beginning boundary nodes $N_b$ and ending boundary nodes $N_e$ in $G$ and a set of predicates $p_i$ such that the time line of the resulting story lies between $T_S = min(start\_time(N_b))$ and $T_E = max(end\_time(N_e))$ such that $T_S < T_E$, and the predicates $p_i$ must be satisfied by the resulting story graph $G_s$. Specifically, a predicate $p_i$ can be a node predicate $p_n$, a connectivity predicate $p_c$ or an aggregate predicate $p_{agg}$. A node predicate must be satisfied by one or more nodes in $G_s$, a connectivity predicate must be satisfied by a single edge, a path or a subgraph of $G_s$ and an aggregate predicate must be satisfied by $G_s$ or any of its component subgraphs. We will describe how the story graph $G_s$ is constructed in several stages. The basic task of the storytelling application is to identify fragments of the event graph that can serve as candidates to be included in the final story. We call these graph fragments as **story components**. Thus, given a story request $Q$ on a graph $G$ an ontology $O(G)$ and a social network $N$, the goal of the storytelling task is to identify a set of story components that can be connected together by the story authors. A story component is a *connected* graph $G_C = \{V_C, E_C, L_C\}$ such that 1) $G_C$ is a subgraph of $G \cup O(G) \cup N$, 2) $G_C$ itself qualifies as an event graph under the same ontology $O(G)$, 3) the time bounds of the events in $G_C$ lie between $T_S$ and $T_E$, 4) $G_C$ satisfies at least some of the predicates in $Q$ and violates none, and 5) $G_C$ is *minimal* in the sense that there is no subgraph of $G_C$ which satisfies the predicates of $Q$.

To illustrate the notion of a story component, let us consider the event graph shown in Fig. 5.1, and the request for "a story for my journalist friend Joseph about interesting personalities I met during my last two trips abroad." Although not shown in the figure, let us assume that all the declared properties of the meeting events are included in the graph. For example, the author's participation in these events is not shown. Let us also assume that the social network associated with the event graph includes the facts that Bill Gates is the former CEO of Microsoft and the founder of the Gates Foundation. The dashed (and red) part of the graph is a minimal description of the graph (i.e., a story component) in response to the query; the component can be paraphrased as "I visited a polio-eradication meeting where Bill Gates participated. He also participated with me in a meeting with the villagers afterwards." Notice that while the subevents of the `polio-eradication meeting` is not part of the story component, the *subevent* relationship between the `meeting with villagers` and the `visit` events is included in it because Bill Gates' possible participation in the subevents of the `polio-eradication meeting` is inferrable, but his participation in the `meeting with villagers` event establishes a separate connection between the author's visit and Bill Gates that must be explicitly included. We include the essential properties of any event included in the story component because we need to preserve the ontological character of the component graph. For now, we ask the reader to intuitively verify that if any edge of the story component is eliminated, the component will lose its value. However, sometimes, just the "minimal" graph may not satisfy the requirement that the results must be ontologically valid. In this case, "Bill Gates" must be put in the ontological context of the story request about "interesting personalities." This will prompt the story component to add in a minimal level of information about Bill Gates as part of the response.

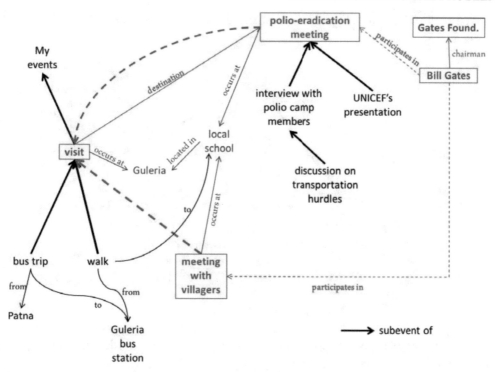

**Figure 5.1:** A simplified event graph where the event author attends a polio eradication meeting where he/she meets a prominent personality. Many properties like the event duration and other participants are omitted in this diagram. We do not show that the bus trip is followed by the walk, followed by the meeting, followed by the meeting with villagers. The part of the event graph shown in dashed red lines is a story component in response to a story request. The part in solid blue are some of the declared properties of the events included in the story component.

This additional information is the edge labeled "chairman" and the node labeled "Gates Found." in Figure 5.1.

Our next step in the process of specifying the story graph $G_s$ is to define a temporal ordering over a story component. The problem of temporal ordering of the nodes of a graph have been investigated by different researchers [Bramsen et al., 2006, Kostakos, 2009]. The goal of our temporal ordering is to logically rearrange a story component graph $G_C$ into an alternate representation $G'_C$ such that 1) each non-leaf event node in $G_C$ are ordered by the temporal relationship *follows*, 2) if event node $e_2$ is a subevent of node $e_1$, and both are in $G_C$, then two new nodes, $e_{1s}, e_{1e}$, representing the start and end of the superevent $e_1$ are introduced, and the *follows* relationship is used to specify the temporal order, 3) all non-event nodes are logically replicated to such that two events are only connected by the *follows* edge. Figure 5.2 shows the temporally ordered equivalent of the story graph from Figure 5.1.

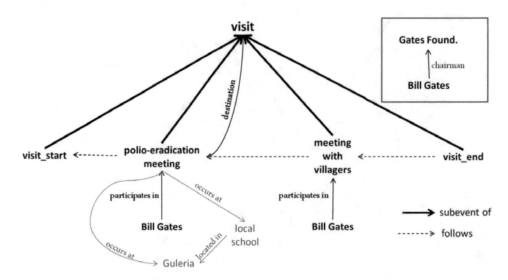

**Figure 5.2:** The story component from Figure 5.1 rearranged for temporal ordering. The declared properties for the second event are omitted for clarity.

As shown in this graph, the non-event property *participates-in* is repeated between two leaf-level events. Also notice that the ontological fragment of the graph has been separated away from the temporally ordered graph as a "contextual" information that accompanies the rest of the ordered story component. In this simple example, the *follows* backbone of the ordered story component is linear; in general, however, it can be a directed acyclic graph because the story component needs to represent concurrent events. Further, the temporal ordering itself can be done in different ways. Bramsen et al. [2006] use the starting time of an event to perform the ordering, while Kostakos [2009] uses a time-division based ordering where the events are first decomposed into to smallest granularity of time and then event nodes are repeated for events that continue over consecutive time granules. Both of these schemes are legal ordering schemes because they uniquely assign a temporal order over a set of events. We state the following without proof.

**Assertion 3** *Given a legal ordering function, any event graph can be temporally reordered.*

Therefore, any story component can be temporally reordered. Without any loss of generality, it can be said that a story component can be modeled as a *two-terminal graph* – if a component graph has multiple roots (or leaves), they can be connected to a single terminal node.

Given a story request $Q$ on an event graph $G$, a number of temporally-ordered story components will match the request. The goal of a storytelling system is to arrange these components in a way that they satisfy all conditions in $Q$, including, potentially a budget constraint on the size of the story graph $G_s$. If the components are disconnected, or if the story author wants to annotate the components, a story component can be complemented with additional *annotation nodes* such that these nodes can explain the component or bridge the gap between disjoint components. In general, there is no unique way of constructing a story graph given its components. However, a number of heuristics can be used for ranking components, selecting components to use toward a story, or creating a story that optimizes some utility function. In Section 5.3, we will look at a few such algorithms.

## 5.2    A STORY REQUEST LANGUAGE

In the last chapter, we discussed a logical language and algebraic operators for querying event graphs, but we did not present a specific surface language. In this section, we sketch the structure of a surface level language that specifies a story request. We will present elements of this language by breaking down the elements of a story graph that a user can specify.

**The Aboutness Clause.** The *aboutness clause* is the central element of a story request that specifies the primary subject matter of the story. The simplest story request will only ask for a story about a set of explicit events ("what happened on my birthday this year"), a time range ("what happened in 2010"), a location range ("story of Coronado Island") or a set of entities ("story on Babbage's computers"). For the simplest query, this is the only required clause. Thus,

```
construct story S {
from myEvents, eventOntology
about (
event(label="polio-eradication-meeting", year='2010')
)
}
```

represents the structure of a basic request. The `construct` clause gives a name to the story. The `from` clause specifies the event graph from which the story will be constructed, as well as the ontology to be used along with. The `about` clause specifies that the central element of the story should be an event, with a conjunctive filtering condition. The construction `event(...)` specifies that the type of the object for this request is an event (and not, for example, a person). In the language, this "tag" can be any entity type recognized in the specified ontology. Notice that while the ontology is mentioned in the request, there is no explicit "join"' clause that directly utilizes it; similarly, there is no "return" clause that specifies exactly what needs to be returned. This illustrates two primary differences between a standard query and a story request – in the case of the latter, the system needs to determine what should be returned and ensure that the resulting story is valid according to the ontology specified. If we wanted the story to be about what Bill Gates did at the meeting, the about clause will be written:

```
about (
person(name='Bill Gates'), event(label="polio-eradication-meeting",
year='2010')
)
```

The semantics of the conjunction is that the story is about both Bill Gates and the meeting. We could further refine the query to state the following:

```
about (
activity(actor.name='Bill Gates') during
(event(label="polio-eradication-meeting", year='2010'))
)
```

Recall from our basic event model that activity is a special kind of event. The `during` connective puts a temporal restriction on the about clause. The difference between this query and the previous one is subtle. If Bill had spoken at a press conference before the meeting day, it will be reported for the first request but not for the second request because the activity did not occur during the meeting event.

**Patterns.** In the examples so far, the request only has an aboutness clause that captures simple topics. In a more complex case, the story will involve a larger cluster of events, entities, locations and time ranges. Consider the following request:

```
about (
event(label="polio-eradication-meeting"|label="meeting with villagers",
year='2010'),
start-story(activity(type='arrival', actor.name='Bill Gates')),
end-story(activity(type='departure', actor.name='Bill Gates'))
)
```

The OR condition on labels is one way to specify multiple events to be covered within a story. The `start-story` and `end-story` clauses limit the time boundaries on the story. The boundaries can be specified by explicit specification of date-time or indirectly, through events.

**The Emphasis Clause.** A special characteristic of the story request language is that it can ask the underlying system to *highlight* certain aspects of the story. In our example, we can say:

```
about (
activity(actor.name='Bill Gates') during
(event(label="polio-eradication-meeting", year='2010'))
)
emphasis(
conversation(participant.name='Bill Gates', participant.organization='UNICEF')
```

This request sends a hint to the underlying algorithm is the all conversation events where both Bill Gates and members of UNICEF participated should have a higher priority when constructing the story. The body of the emphasis clause is a comma separated set of events. One can think of an extension where these events have user-defined weights specified.

**The Exclusion Clause.** The exclusion clause has the same structure as the emphasis clause and explicitly disallows certain events from being included in the story.

```
about (
activity(actor.name='Bill Gates') during
```

```
(event(label="polio-eradication-meeting", year='2010'))
)
exclude(
activity(participant.name='Bill Gates') during event(type='lunch'))
```

The exclusion clause prohibits the inclusion of any activity that occurred during the time interval that has been labeled 'lunch'.

**The Audience Clause.** The optional audience clause is an expression that specifies a set of individuals on a social network. The simplest expression in the audience clause can be an enumerated set of entities in the social network. In a general case, we need to use a language to express to perform a node selection. All nodes in the network are specified relative to the distinguished node called 'myself', representing the identity of the requester. The social relationships used in the social network can come from any ontology like foaf[1] or the relationship ontology[2]. The following expression selects the parents and parents-in-law of the entity 'myself'.

```
construct story S {
from myEvents, eventOntology, mySocialNetwork
...
audience(
myself.childOf union myself.spouseOf.childOf
)
}
```

**Using Joins.** So far, we have avoided explicit joins within a clause or between different clauses of a story request. Sometimes, however, it is necessary to use explicit join clauses to link different objects specified in the different parts of the request. Suppose we would like to get a story of all people who participated in discussions with members of the UNICEF. We can specify this:

```
about (
activity((actor.name=$X) during
(event(label="polio-eradication-meeting", year='2010'))
where exists conversation(participant.name=$X, participant.organization='UNICEF')
)
```

using explicit join variables. As in many query languages, the `where` clause can be used inside any other clause (e.g., the aboutness clause here) as well as within the body of the query where the join involves variables from multiple clauses.

**The Limit Clause.** In most cases where the event graph is large or the part of the graph contributing to the story is large, one needs to provide a "budget." The budget is always specified as a limit clause that specifies the minimum or the maximum number of events, entities, nodes, total graph size, total number of media objects and so forth that should be included in the story. Multiple limits may be placed on a single story request. However, these limits are "soft" because it is an algorithmically hard optimization problem to exactly maintain all the limits strictly and yet produce a story that satisfies

[1] http://xmlns.com/foaf/spec/
[2] http://vocab.org/relationship/.html

all other criteria. The algorithms for maintaining the limits is an open research problem beyond the scope of these lectures.

**Multimedia.** Multimedia objects have a special role in storytelling. In many cases, the popularity or importance of an event is indicated by the number of multimedia objects associated with it. Sometimes the author of events would post media objects that are not (yet) associated with any events. In these cases, one can consider the time density of media capture events – the high density regions provide time fragments that are important and can hence be used to indirectly infer the importance of events falling within those time periods. The storytelling request language provides a number of hints on how media objects should be chosen for the story. All of these hints fall in the `limits` clause.

```
limits(
count(image(any event)) < 3,
count(image.designates("Bill Gates")) < 2,
count(image(S)) < 20,
aggregate_image(subevents) = true
)
```

The first limit uses the qualifier `any` to state that no single event represented in the story can have more than 2 pictures. If an event and its superevent are both part of the story, the constraint applies to both. To exclude the superevent from this restriction, one can refine the condition to `any leaf event` instead. The second option refers to images that have been explicitly "tagged" with the name of a person. The third constraint uses is on `S`, the whole story graph. The last constraint allows that a superevent can aggregate all images from its subevents. This is especially useful when only the superevent is included in the story as in the case of Figure 5.1.

A second way to use multimedia is to create a "cartoon" story where a story is constructed by creating a temporal sequence of images, where each image depicts a story event, and the sequencing of media is a way of linearizing the ordered story elements computed from the events. To produce such a story, one simply alters the `construct` clause of the request to `construct multimedia story S`. In the next section, we will show how such a story is constructed.

## 5.3   ALGORITHMS FOR STORYTELLING

To process a story request, a story computing system will have to go through the following steps (although some of the steps may need to be reordered for more efficient execution).

1. select events, people, etc., that satisfy the aboutness clause, and mark them as *candidate anchor nodes*

2. using constraints and filtering conditions, determine the starting and ending time intervals for the requested story

3. construct *candidate story components* by propagating from the candidate anchor nodes to their neighborhoods while satisfying the requirements for the emphasis and exclusion criteria

```
construct story S {
from myEvents E, eventOntology O, DBpediaOntology D, mySocialNetwork N
about (
meeting(E.participant='myself', (E.participant.name=D.people.name |
E.participant.organization=D.organization.name ) during
trip(E.participant='myself', E.destination.country != 'USA', E.occurs_during='2010'),
)
emphasis(exists image(E.witness))
exclude(meeting(E.private='true'))
audience($X=N.myself.friend , ($X.profession='journalist' |
$X.profession='reporter'))
limits(
count(image(any leaf event)) < 3,
count(image.designates(D.people.name)) < 2,
count(event(S)) < 40,
aggregate_image(subevents) = true
) }
```

Figure 5.3: A full story request.

4. extract from the story request, the *minimal ontological profile* required for each node of the candidate story components

5. augment the candidate story components by joining them with ontology fragments and social networks as needed for each significant node. The information nodes added this way will be called *context nodes*, and the network added with be called the *context graph*.

6. rank the primary nodes of each story components to meet the minimality and budget requirements

7. rank the component graphs in terms of their relevance to the story request

8. determine which component graphs should be composed together to form the story

9. choose the media elements that should be included in the final story

10. create the ordered story components for this graph, allow the user to interject annotation nodes, and output the highest ranking story. In the case of a media story, the ordered story components will be ordering the media objects.

To illustrate these steps in detail, consider a variant of our example request for "a story for my journalist friends about interesting personalities I met during my last year's trip abroad." Figure 5.3 shows the query in the request language in the previous section.

In this query, we use a simplified definition of "interesting personalities" as any person who is listed in DBpedia Ontology or people who are employed by well known organizations. We can get this information from the DBPedia Ontology, which is based on OWL and describes classes like person, organization, city, country, and properties, like birthplace and longitude. We also would like to emphasize events where images were captured (i.e., events that have a `witness` property of the type 'image') but exclude events that are marked as private meetings.

**Generating Candidate Anchors.** To generate the candidate anchor nodes, we must evaluate the two predicates regarding trips and meetings temporally joined through the `during` connective. A simple optimization rule determines that the predicates within the during clause should be evaluated first, and amongst the predicates therein, a predicate giving absolute time boundaries for the entire story should be evaluated earliest. A second optimization can be performed on the exclusion clause. Since the exclusion criterion involves a condition only on an event property, the query is reformulated to eliminate the exclusion clause and move the exclusion predicate within the about clause. However, before evaluating for trips in 2010, the algorithm needs to account for the fact that "trip" as an entity type may have subtypes, and hence the selection should retrieve to all direct and inherited instances of "my trips" in 2010. This query is facilitated by the `SSJoinTable` bitmap index that would encode the expression (`?trip participant 'myself'`)(`?trip year 2010`). As the 2010 trips get identified, it provides the opportunity to perform a semantic query optimization by providing an additional set of temporal filters (corresponding to the time bounds of these trips) to the predicates involving direct and indirect instances of `meeting`, so that every meeting that is evaluated will need to pass through them. The join condition between the set of event participants and the set of people from DBPediaOntology can be implemented by any standard join techniques like merge join. As the set of trips $Tr$ and corresponding meetings $M$ are identified by filtering the other predicates, these nodes, together with their set of qualifying participants $P$, are included in the candidate anchor set $A$. Notice that to find the anchor points for this request, we combine several stages of the story processing outline.

**Adding the Context Graph.** In figure 5.2, we designated the edge (`"Bill Gates" chairman "Gates Foundation"`) as contextual information added to our search because it is relevant for the request involving "interesting personalities." An algorithm trying to add such context nodes for a request needs to address two questions: 1) "which context nodes (e.g., Bill Gates? UNICEF's representative?) should be added," and 2) "what information related to these context nodes (e.g., "Gates Foundation?" Microsoft?) should be added." To facilitate context graph extraction, the previous step for anchor node detection must be refined as follows. For each predicate in the request, identify the entities and properties from the ontologies that reference the anchor nodes. In example query, the anchor nodes are event participants, and the referred properties are their organizations. For each identified candidate anchor node, maintain a list of these properties and property values, some of which will be entities themselves (e.g., a person or an organization). Rank these entities using a suitable criterion and accept the top $k$ items. In our case, a suitable rank may be obtained by a *Google score* defined as

$$\frac{\log(hits\ in\ Google)}{\log(total\ number\ of\ Google\ pages)}$$

However, the choice of this function and the value of $k$ are application dependent. Next, we need to explore the ontology (in this case DBPedia) to construct the contextual graph. Using a similar strategy as before, one can construct a contextual scoring function based on the Normalized Google

Distance [Cilibrasi and Vitányi, 2007, Gligorov et al., 2007].

$$NGD(x, y) = \frac{max(\log f(x), \log f(y)) - log f(x, y)}{log M - min(\log f(x), \log f(y))}$$

where

$f(x)$ = number of Google hits for term $x$

$f(y)$ = number of Google hits for term $y$

$f(x, y)$ = number of Google hits for terms $x$ and $y$ together

$M$ = number of pages indexed by Google

To apply this formula, we propagate from the terms representing the pruned candidate anchor nodes (e.g., "Bill Gates") within the ontology and along the properties (e.g., organization) and select the values of these properties (e.g., Microsoft, "Gates Foundation"). These context terms $c_i$ correspond to the term $x$ in the formula. The term $y$ of the formula comes from the event itself. Thus, the polio-eradication-meeting is about polio, eradication, and "polio eradication;" these event terms $e_j$ are used as the $y$ term. Thus, we compute $max_i(max_j(NGD(c_i, e_j)))$ and choose the $c_i$ terms that serves as the maximum term. In this case, the "Gates Foundation" will be more relevant to polio than "Microsoft." Note that here we just used the ontological properties that appear in the query (i.e., organization); in a more general case, one can relax this requirement and recursively compute the distance metric for all properties propagating out from the candidate anchor node and define a stopping criterion based on a threshold or a significant drop-off in contextual relevance. Once these terms are identified from the ontology, we add the propagation path from the anchor nodes to the selected ontology nodes.

**Generating Candidate Story Components.** To construct the candidate story components from the context-augmented candidate anchor node, we need to navigate and select a suitable subgraph from the event graph. The nature of this navigation depends on the search strategy, and must factor additional parameters including the impact of the audience, the role of the multimedia content, and the budget restrictions on the overall result size. The algorithm runs in several phases. The first phase finds disjoint subgraphs from the event graph such that each subgraph covers some subset of the candidate anchor nodes, they collectively cover all anchor nodes, and the maximal time distance between consecutive parts of the same subgraph is less than a threshold $\tau$. A number of techniques can be employed to extract these subgraphs. A simple technique that works well in practice uses an *anchor distance matrix* (Table 5.1, a symmetric matrix whose rows and columns represent the anchor nodes ordered in time, and each cell value $d(i, j)$ contains the temporal distance between the $i$-th and the $j$-th anchor nodes. Since the nodes are time ordered, the temporal distances in each row will be monotonic nondecreasing. We can use this fact to find column boundaries that show discontinuities larger than $\tau$ consistently for all rows. In Table 5.1, nodes 1-5 form a group while nodes 6-7 form another. This would translate to a rough separation of the event graph into two regions, the first from the start time of anchor node 1 till the end time of anchor node 5, and the second, from the start time of anchor node 6 till the end of anchor node 7. These "cut out" portions of the event graph are called *covering segments* over anchor clusters. This is a simple algorithm for finding clusters around constellations of anchor nodes. In practice, more complex clustering algorithms might be needed to find clean cluster separations.

Table 5.1: The upper half of the anchor distance matrix with 7 anchor nodes and $\tau=4$.

| Node | 1 | 2 | 3 | 4 | 5 | 6 | 7 |
|---|---|---|---|---|---|---|---|
| 1 | 0 | 1 | 2 | 4 | 5 | 13 | 15 |
| 2 | | 0 | 2 | 2 | 4 | 10 | 13 |
| 3 | | | 0 | 3 | 9 | 11 | 14 |
| 4 | | | | 0 | 3 | 9 | 11 |
| 5 | | | | | 0 | 2 | 3 |
| 6 | | | | | | 0 | 2 |
| 7 | | | | | | | 0 |

Once the time boundaries for the individual story components are determined, the next task is actually construct the component story graphs by using the neighborhoods of the anchor nodes. We describe two "greedy" strategies for the construction.

***Using Audience Preferences.*** In this strategy, we assume that each member of the social network is associated with a set of typed preferences. For example, a journalist might be interested in economics in general and foreign investment in particular, another may be interested in rural health issues in general and child health in particular. Satish et al. [2009] model audience interest as a set of weighted preference list $P(m) = \{(N_i(m), w_i(m)\}$ for each member $m$ of the social network $N$. The algorithm first determines the audience by evaluating audience clause from the story request and extracts their preference lists. Then it attempts to compute the scores of events based on the audience preference list so that events having property names or property values that are similar to the terms in the user's preference lists are weighted higher. To this end, it defines an *event interestingness* measure as

$$I_e(e_i) = \sum_{S_i \in e_i} (w_i)$$

$I_e(e_i)$ is normalized by the number of maximum number of attributes an event instance might have from the events in the candidate anchor set. We can now use the node interestingness measures to define a notion of *story interestingness*. Suppose the algorithm has processed $i$ nodes so far. Let $S_T$ is the complete story with $T$ events. Satish et al. [2009] introduce the notion of *story interestingness* $I(S_T)$, which is the story counterpart of event interestingness. Let $I_e(e_i|S_{i-1})$ be the contribution to the story interestingness by the event $e_i$ given that $S_{i-1}$

is the story component graph constructed so far. So,

$$I(S_i) = I(S_{i-1}) + I_e(e_i | S_{i-1})$$

where

$$I(S_0) = initial$$

$$I_e(e_i | S_{i-1}) = \begin{cases} 0 & \text{when } e_i \in S_{i-1} \\ I_e(e_i) & \text{otherwise} \end{cases}$$

The goal of this storytelling algorithm is to choose the events in such a way that it keeps the story interestingness as high as possible. This basic strategy can be refined in various ways. First, user preference is only one criterion to define event interestingness. Other factors contributing to it can be a normalized number of aggregated media objects per image, the number of personalities met, the number of conversation events, the length of conversation descriptions (recall the emphasis on conversation events) and so forth. Also recall that since the resulting story component must be ontologically sound, the story component graph must include mandatory properties of each type of event according to the ontology. Further, the algorithm can be modified to reduce the total number of nodes in the story, for example, by using higher-level events to replace the lower level events if needed.

***Using Event Transitions.*** A different consideration to construct story components should be applied for covering segments that are dense. Inspired by how comic stories are created, a transitions based scheme for storytelling has been developed by Eisner [2005], McCloud [1993] and Satish et al. [2010]. Transitions are changes, defined by the following classes.

- **Moment-To-Moment Transition**: This occurs when the two events occurred very close to each other, and hence, their content varies very little.

- **Participant-To-Participant Transition**: This involves a transition where both the events contain different participants within the same context (idea). The events must not too be too far apart in space and time.

- **Action To Action Transition**: This occurs when the transition between the two events show a semantic change in actions being performed by the participant. For example, if an event describes Tim starting a car, and the next one describes him driving on the street within a few minutes of the first event, then we can associate an action to action transition.

- **Scene-To-Scene Transition**: This occurs when the two adjacent events occur in different locations or distant time. Such a transition denotes the end of a particular idea in the message and the start of another. They can be far apart in time and space. If two events demonstrate this transition, there must be not be any other transition between events before the first events and those of the event after the second event.

- **Aspect-To-Aspect Transition**: These occur between media of descriptive nature. They describe different aspects of a location. The idea is to describe a certain location and the different objects in it.

- **Other Transitions**: McCloud classifies these as Non-Sequitur transitions. In effect, these are random transitions between events when they have no direct relationships with one another.

In practical applications, participant and action transitions are used more often than the other transitions. Satish et al. [2010] approach the story component construction problem in the following manner. Let the set of events in the system be denoted as $\{E\}$. The set of events which do not have experiential data, (superevents) be denoted as $\{E\}_s$. The set of events whose sole purpose is to record the event which led to the creation of the experiential data is denoted as $\{E\}_x$. Thus, the event set $\{E\}$ is composed of $\{E\}_s$ and $\{E\}_x$ and edges between them. Effectively, we can look at $\{E\}$ as a set of trees where the root is always from $\{E\}_s$ and leaves from $\{E\}_x$. Trees can refer to each other using non-subevent labels.

A story component is a single tree. The root node is a story node, $e_{st}$. Its children, which are also the leaf level, there exist a set of events with experiential data $L_x$. Also, in the story tree, between each adjacent events from the $\{E\}_x$ set, there exists a transition edge. We indicate moment transitions as $T_m$, participant transitions as $T_p$, action transitions as $T_a$, aspect transitions as $T_{as}$, scene transitions as $T_s$ and finally other transitions as $T_o$. The transitions set, $T_x$ is denoted as follows:

$$T_x = [T_m, T_p, T_a, T_{as}, T_s, T_o]$$

For each anchor event, $e$ there is an episode, $e_p$ under the story node. Also, the list of leaf events under the episodes are a subset of $\{E\}_x$, where e is an ancestor of $\{E\}_x$. In order to determine the transition relationships between the events $\{E\}_x$, we use the operator $T(\{E\}_x)$. We compute each of the transitions in the $T$ independently.

A **moment transition** is discovered between two adjacent events, when they have the same participant, performing the same action, and the difference in time between the two is very small.

$$T_m(E_x) \xrightarrow{\delta t} E_x + T_a$$

Specifically, for two events $e_1$ and $e_2$ in $\{E\}_x$, we can write the following:

$$t_m(e_1, e_2) = true, \text{ if and only if} \tag{5.1}$$

$$PARENT(e_1) = PARENT(e_2), \text{ and}$$

$$e_1.P = e_2.P, \text{ and}$$

$$e_1.A = e_2.A, \text{ and}$$

$$|e_2.T - e_1.T| < \delta t.$$

An **action transition** is defined where for each event, we are able to find the next event within the same subevent which has the same participant. Also, the time difference $\delta t$ between the events must be relatively small.

$$T_a(E_x) \xrightarrow{\delta t} E_x + T_a$$

Specifically, for two events $e_1$ and $e_2$ in $\{E\}_x$, we can write the following:

$$t_a(e_1, e_2) = true, \text{ if and only if} \tag{5.2}$$

$$PARENT(e_1) = PARENT(e_2), \text{ and}$$

$$e_1.P = e_2.P, \text{ and}$$

$$e_1.A \neq e_2.A, \text{ and}$$

$$|e_2.T - e_1.T| < \delta t.$$

where, $t_a$ is a function which determines if an action transition exists between $e_1$ and $e_2$. $P$, $A$ are the Participant and corresponding Action set for the event. $\delta t$ is a user supplied parameter.

A **participant transition**, where for each event, within the time bound $\delta t$, another event exists where the participant is different, but the event is under the same subevent.

$$T_p(E_x) \xrightarrow{\delta t} E_x + T_p$$

Specifically, for two events $e_1$ and $e_2$ in $\{E\}_x$, we can write the following:

$$t_p(e_1, e_2) = true, \text{ if and only if} \tag{5.3}$$

$$PARENT(e_1) = PARENT(e_2), \text{ and}$$

$$e_1.P \neq e_2.P, \text{ and}$$

$$|e_2.T - e_1.T| < \delta t.$$

where, $t_a$ is a function which determines if an action transition exists between $e_1$ and $e_2$. $P$ is the Participant set for the event. $\delta t$ is a user supplied parameter.

A **scene transition** occurs, when two events in $\{E\}_x$ do not share the same ancestor.

$$T_s(E_x) \rightarrow E_x + T_s$$

Specifically, for two events $e_1$ and $e_2$ in $\{E\}_x$, we can write the following:

$$t_s(e_1, e_2) = true, \text{ if and only if} \tag{5.4}$$

$$PARENT(e_1) \neq PARENT(e_2), \text{ and}$$

where, $t_a$ is a function which determines if a scene transition exists between $e_1$ and $e_2$. McCloud [1993] defines all the events as **aspect transitions**, which describe the environment in which the current event is taking place. An aspect transition can occur between two event sequences if they occur in two different environments. Since environment is a global parameter, it is necessary that environment is computed over a sequence of events rather than a single event. Aspects are media properties rather than event properties. Effectively in finding a best set of aspect transitions, we are trying to find the right set of media elements which describe the environment under consideration visually. Specifically, for two event sequences $E_1$ and $E_1$ in $\{E\}_x$, we can write the following:

$$t_{sp}(E_1, E_2) = true, \text{ if and only if} \tag{5.5}$$

if:

$$E_1.LOCATION = E_2.LOCATION, \text{ and}$$

$$E_1.Media.LOCATION \neq E_2.Media.LOCATION.$$

With all the transitions computed, we obtain the set of leaf events in the story as follows:

$$L_x = E_x + T_a + T_p + T_s + T_{sp} - T_m \tag{5.6}$$

Finally, the story component is constructed by running an interestingness algorithm over the neighborhoods of these leaf nodes. Once these events are identified, their essential properties are added, making it an ontologically correct graph.

A proper story component finding algorithm will possibly combine these two strategies. It will also enforce all size constraints except for the global size content. Thus, it will choose representative images when a large number of images can be associated with an event. How these images are selected is outside the scope of these lecture notes. Further, notice that the candidate story component graph is not minimized at this point, and it is deferred till the next step where we address constraints on the overall size of the result.

**Pruning the Story Component Graphs.** After all candidate story component graphs are created and their total size exceeds the total size budget for the story, one must evaluate the importance of each story component graph to determine whether and how it needs to be reduced in the final story. First, the overall graph budget $B$ is apportioned into story component budgets $b_i$, based on some properties of the component graphs. A simple way to assign the budget would be to break them in proportion to the component size. This, however, can be misleading because a larger component may have more extraneous content that can possibly be pruned. A better method is to assign the budget according to the relative interestingness of the components. Given a budget $b_i$, three potential actions can be taken to reduce the size of the component – 1) replacing a set of lower nodes along the subevent hierarchy by a single higher node, 2) merging a subgraph into a single node, and 3) pruning a node and its edges.

- *Event Node Replacement.* In the trivial case, an event node $e$ replaces its subevent nodes $e_1, \ldots e_n$ if all $n$ child nodes are selected by the previous algorithms. More generally, however, event node replacement is based on an assessment of how the replacement will impact the overall interestingness and structure of the story component. The loss of interestingness can be considered as a cost function based upon the difference between the original interestingness $I(S)$ and the modified interestingness $I(S')$ after the substitution. For example, the structure of the story component is affected if removing an existing node $e_i$ results in the removal of an edge $(e_i \, label \, e_{n+1})$, and there is no direct path from the superevent node $e$ to the node $e_{n+1}$. To connect $e$ to $e_{n+1}$, one has to construct a *legal* edge between these nodes, by following a set of rules. For example, if *label* = 'caused', and $e$ occurs before $e_{n+1}$, a rule might allow the construction of an edge $e \, partly \, causes \, e_{n+1}$. It is possible to associate a *repair cost* with the inclusion of the new edge.

- *Subgraph Condensation.* The problem of subgraph condensation has been addressed by researchers performing graph summarization [Navlakha et al., 2008, Tian et al., 2008b, Zhang et al., 2010]. These algorithms do construct aggregated nodes by combining nodes of similar nature or nodes connected by similar links, but their emphasis is on constructing a compact representation of a given graph [Navlakha et al., 2008], or on creating a summary that reflects the patterns of connection in a large graph by looking at node properties and edge labels. The primary distinction between their motivation and storytelling is that they do not need to take into account any external node weights assigned by non-structural factors such as the user's preference or the semantics of transitions. Our approach to the problem is to define a set of rules that defines different conditions for node merging and the cost of the operations. For example, a rule might state that all events of the type conversation can be merged if they are between the same parties and all within a specified time limit, and the interestingness of the merged node will be the weighted sum of their individual interestingness values, such that the weights are proportional to the duration of the event. Given a set of such rules, the task of the pruning algorithm is to achieve the maximum condensation with a minimal loss of interestingness.

- *Node Pruning.* In the previous cases, nodes that were removed from the story graph were either aggregated or substituted. In the case of pruning, the node is completely removed. In some situations, the pruning will not affect the story component significantly. For example, if ten consecutive events have the same location, then the location of the last nine events can removed, so long as the next story event happening at a different location is specified. As in the case of event replacement, node pruning is also associated with a loss of interestingness cost and a repair cost.

The overall budget constraint problem can therefore be stated as an optimization problem where the graph modifications must restrict the number of nodes to within a fixed bound $\epsilon$ of the budget while keeping the total cost at a minimum.

**Generating the Final Story.** After the reduced story components are computed, they are temporally ordered, and tested for gaps. The gaps might be temporal, locational or thematic and are determined by a number of control directives that determine how a story is constructed. These directives include (a) the maximum allowed temporal gap between two consecutive story components, (b) whether a gap in the locations of events within a story component or in the locations of two consecutive story components are allowed (they can be allowed in a travel story, but not in a meeting story), (c) whether a discontinuity between the participants (or any other property) of two consecutive events (vis-a-vis story components) is allowed, (d) the ontological consistency of a story component or across story components (e.g., are all events within a component about a trip?), and (e) whether the full story is allowed to have temporally parallel components. If a generated story does not adhere to one or more of these directives, the story creator has to create annotation nodes to "hold together" the story for the final recipient.

CHAPTER 6

# An Emerging Application

In this chapter, we will discuss an application of event information system that is shaping up to play increasingly important role in our society. This application has been talked in many systems for personal media management to defense related applications. An early version of this was commonly called LifeLog. Our goal in this chapter is to present this emerging field, discuss the data collected in this application, and developing systems that can utilize all these data for effective use. Human life, and so any other organism or organization's life, is a sequence of events. The importance of different events varies depending on their nature, length, and impact on other events in life. Historically, people have used different mechanisms to record information and experiences related to events. This process started with personal memory. As technology developed, humans always used the most modern technology of their time to record their personal experiences of events either to share with others, or to relive them, or to reflect upon and understand events and relationships. This process of recording important events and experiences associated with them started on cave walls and has closely tracked the technology evolution since then. Personal diaries, autobiographies, biographies, chronicles, photo albums, video collections, and lifelogs using cameras and other devices demonstrate how with changing technologies, mechanisms for recording experiences have changed. Electronic media has brought interesting new dimensions to this art of recording personal experiences for sharing and reflecting. First, it has now become extremely easy to record such experiences with almost zero effort. Different sensors in mobile phones can record location, time, and activity information unobtrusively. Many other sensors are becoming part of mobile phones and will even record health related information. Combine these with camera and microphones in the phones and you have powerful audio-visual experience capture for events. Effectively, we are now at a point when we can record a significant part of our life using sensors in a mobile phone. Since most people have their mobile phone always with them, data related to all events in which one participated is being recorded mostly in the background. Moreover, people record some other important data effortlessly using camera and microphone in the phone. The ease of collection of personal activity related data has resulted in many research projects and many companies that are recording data related to some activity, say eating habits or physical activities, and providing applications that track and analyze this data for personal improvements. It is expected that future health care will depend a lot on such applications.

The second aspect of collecting these data is that the volume and types of data pose new data management challenges. The data from different sources usually result in different silos that do not communicate with each other and are indexed using data centric approaches. In the current form, it is not possible to make sense of these diverse sources of data. We believe that by organizing all this data around meaningful events, it is possible to understand data to reflect on broader experiences of events and then share and reflect on them. Business intelligence emerged out of desire to correlate different data sources for analyzing focused business events for taking data-supported actions. We believe that time has come to develop actionable personal intelligence techniques using the data being continuously collected by our phones and other devices.

Suppose that using different data sources, one can segment time into events and associate different sensory data as well as actions like mail and phone calls with such events. These events are then used for organizing and managing all data. Also events can be easily classified into meaningful event-types such as personal, family, professional, social, and spiritual. By organizing all data related to a person in such events, one can then also do very rigorous analysis to obtain information related to health conditions, professional and personal relationships, and any other aspects that may be desired. This data is the richest source of objective information about a person and can be explored to provide actionable personal intelligence to the person.

The techniques discussed in this book are directly related to this application. Lets discuss this application scenario more concretely. Suppose that we have a system that combines data from different sources, including mobile phones and many sensors that are increasingly appearing in these phones, and creates a log of data about the person. Let us consider that among all other data, the following data streams are collected ($t$ indicates time and $k$ indicates a series):

- $Location(t)$: The location of the user at regular time interval,

- $P - events$: The set of planned event streams $PE_i$ (time interval, type, location, participants) from calendar and other sources,

- $Photos(k)$: Photo taken by the user (time, location),

- $Audio(k)$: Audio during time-interval $t_k$ (time, location, interval),

- $Video(k)$: Video during time-interval $t_k$ (time, location, interval),

- $HealthIndicator(say BloodPressure)(t)$: Collected at regular time intervals,

- $Accelerometer(t)$: Recorded at regular time intervals,

- $Ambientsound(t)$: Recorded at regular time intervals.

Based on these data streams and models of different events, all this data are used to segment the person's timeline into event structures and associated informational and experiential data. This event structure can be characterized as $E_i$ that covers the timeline. We use a special type of event called Enull to represent the type of unknown event. *Enull* is a catch-all event type that will contain unknown as well as don't care events. Non-null events are of two types: planned events ($PE_i$) and impromptu events ($IE_i$). Planned events can be created by the system using sources such as calendar while impromptu events are detected by events based on models of events.

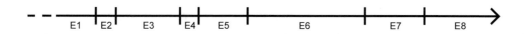

Figure 6.1: Events occupy the timeline. In fact, events are structuralization of the timeline using semantics, rather than the uniform structuralization as imposed by calendars.

Let's consider a life as a collection of events. This perspective allows us to group all observed data at any time instant from any sensor related to the person as experiential data associated with the event taking place at that time. Other people and objects can be considered as part of the informational data related to the event. We show this in Figure 6.1. All experiential data can be analyzed to determine the type of events and even participants in the event. This can also be used to determine the location of the event. In fact, the experiential data is very rich for collecting and analyzing all elements of actionable personal intelligence. Each event on the timeline - or the lifeline - can be an atomic event or could be a composite event. In fact, a composite event may have several non-contiguous events as its component, though it may also have contiguous atomic or composite events as its constituent. Moreover, an event could be part of multiple composite events.

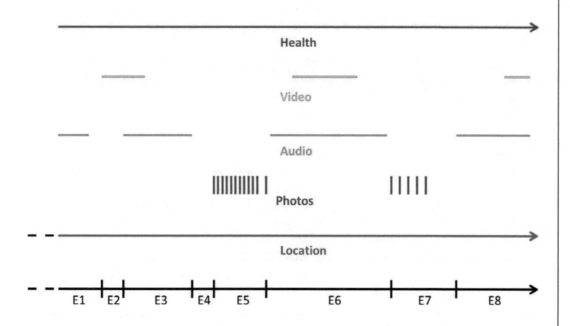

Figure 6.2: Different information and observation sources help in interpretation and population of events. Here we show a few data sources synchronized with the time axis, resulting in easily seeing connections between events and other sources.

Based on different sources of information and the interpretation of the observation, the time line is segmented into events. The observation sources are all organized according to the time and are synchronized with the time axis. This is shown in Figure 6.2 for a few observation and data sources. Note that some data may be continuously available for an object or a person, while other data sources may be available only during certain time instants or time intervals.

Suppose that all this data are stored in PersonXLife. As pointed out by several researchers working on collecting such data and developing techniques to use such data [Gemmell et al., 2006, Lee et al., 2010], all this data could now be used by the person or by somebody else, with appropriate permissions, to analyze and understand this data for recollecting, reflecting, retrieving, recalling, and reminiscing on her life. In particular, one may ask questions like the following:

*Q1*: I misplaced my keys. Let me backtrack my events to think where I could have left them.

*Q2*: My buddy for the last 15 years is getting married. I am supposed to roast him by telling funny incidents and showing embarrassing photos of him. In fact, I may also show how he has grown in this process from a lean and thin guy to his current size.

*Q3*: My relationship with Tom seems to be going through a tough period. Why is that? Are we not spending enough time with each other? Are we not communicating enough? Let me analyze the events in the last 6 months to understand this.

*Q4*: There are some food items that result in discomfort and loss of sleep for me. Let me plot the food eaten and sleep problems for the last six months to see what food I should avoid.

*Q5*: How are the research publications submitted by my students in the last 6 months related to the visits of Visiting Professors in the last two years?

*Q6*: In my international trips, what is the ratio of number of photos taken at sightseeing places to those at conferences? Also, on such trips, how much time I spent sightseeing compared to the time I spent in professional activities.

*Q7*: Show the top 5 people or objects in all my photos.

*Q8*: How and when did I fall in love with Mary? Analyze first 25 events related to my meetings with Mary and give estimates of the time I spent with her and the activities we participated in.

*Q9*: Am I ignoring my family (or profession)? Find quality time I spent with my family in the last 6 months.

*Q10*: There is something odd about this photo that is bothering me. Let me see all data and information related to the photo and the corresponding event and analyze to find what that could be.

**Actionable Personal Intelligence is Event Analytics.** It is easy to see that first by using all data that is logged by an individual in their mobile phone, and through their activities in cyberspace one can first create an information system that uses event models of the kind we discussed in earlier sections. For each event, one has different information as well as experiential data. Moreover, with little curation on the part of user, it is possible to enrich this by relating events and creating a Web of events, as discussed in [Jain, 2008]. Moreover, since all the events and data is available, it will be possible for a person to use this system for recollecting, reflecting, retrieving, recalling, and reminiscing about events and related information and experiences using queries as listed above. It should be stressed that all the queries listed above are very related to the queries discussed in Chapter 4 and can be easily implemented for the system that can be built using techniques discussed in this book.

# CHAPTER 7

# Conclusion

Information systems usually model a perspective of the real world. Early information systems appeared in the form of databases and were primarily concerned with modeling objects and their attributes in the domain of an application. The requirements of these systems could be directly modeled using entities, their relationships, and their attributes using relational algebra. Very efficient techniques were developed to manage these systems even at very large scales. With progress in computing and communication technology, information systems found applications in areas where the models included semi-structured and unstructured data that were not necessarily under the control of the system administrator. The Web created demands on information systems that required serious re-thinking of the approaches that had been so successful in earlier applications.

The rapid advances in computing and communications continue. Emerging systems are increasingly dealing with events in the real world as they happen. Events can be in limited environments, such as databases or a media streams, or they can be in real world where information about them is captured using many different sensors, including human's sensors, and is used to populate event information manually or automatically. For events happening in real world, all the data from various sources are collected and stored. There data are used to get information about events, analyze and understand them, and share experiences around them. Emerging information systems are being asked to support this eco system around events.

In early information systems, events were the changes made in the information systems, with no direct link to the happenings in the world being modeled. Events are naturally related to time. Temporal databases and active databases addressed early concepts in events. Slowly, databases started dealing with data streams and considered that events represent when something of interest happens in the stream. In those cases, only the instant of happening is of interest and all actions are based on that instant. With increasing use of stream data from applications like stock market data, events started becoming more sophisticated and the concept of Complex Event Processing started gaining attention. In Chapter 1, we reviewed approaches developed for event representations and role of events in information systems. We also considered sensor networks and systems where some actions needed to be taken based to the detection of the event. A very important thread in all such applications was that the focus in modeling events was on the time - other aspects of changes were considered secondary. Other information systems that considered events were video and multimedia surveillance systems. In most of these systems, the emphasis was on detecting events based on their video or multimedia attributes. For these systems, similar to the information systems, events were limited in the dataset that these systems considered.

One interesting observation about characterization and use of events in the early systems is similar to the famous fable about 'The blind men and the elephant'. By adopting a limited perspective of events, early systems focused only on some limited aspects of events in applications. In some applications, this is acceptable. Similar to the story of the blind men, however, a perspective of the event may be so limited that it may be wrong. For modeling events as they happen in real world, we must adopt the holistic perspective.

The interface between an information system and real world used to be a human. All information in early system was mediated by a human and contained data that came through humans. Increasingly, information systems are dealing with dynamic evolving world. In the dynamic evolving world, much information may come directly from sensors. Sensors are interface between an information system and the real world that the system is modeling. A very important but often forgotten fact is that sensors are placed only at those locations where something of interest is happening. Such changes should be automatically captured and represented in information systems.

The real world is modeled using objects and events. Objects represent persistent qualities associated with entities of different types. The relationships among objects and their attributes keep changing and are primarily responsible for the dynamic and changing world. Events are used to model these changes. Neither objects alone nor events alone can be effective in modeling the dynamic evolving world. We need both, and we need to represent and model the relationships and changes in relationships among objects and events. We started Chapter 2 by asking the question: "What are we trying to model?" We discussed what aspects of a real world event should be modeled, and how the structure of events should be represented. The role of time and space and their clear representation was discussed here. To represent many different types of events and relationships among events and their sub-events and events and objects, use of ontological approaches was reviewed. Representation of ontological concepts using RDF and their relationships to traditional approaches such as extended entity-relationship model in the context of event representation was discussed. It was also shown that events are not usually independent; they are causally related to other events. Considering all these requirements, some of the recent models used in emerging systems were reviewed.

It is very important to specify and model all important aspects of an event. Following model E, we considered time, space, entities and other attributes, experiential data collected using different sensors, relationship among events and other sub-events as well as events and other events based on causality. We defined model $E^*$ to concretize model E for implementation purposes. We defined mechanisms to specify all these facets or attributes of events and presented formal and precise approaches to define these using appropriate tools drawn from multiple areas ranging from logic and ontology to traditional database systems.

Emerging information systems are increasingly dealing with real world happenings as captured by humans, but also as captured and reported using experiential data such as audio, photos, videos, and many other types of sensors including sophisticated medical sensors. In many systems, latency plays an important role. In these systems, many, if not the most, events must be automatically detected, and the information system should be populated without much, if any, intervention or help from humans. Another major difference was the requirement that event itself should be considered important, and its attributes and relationships with other objects and events should also be modeled and represented. Increasingly, information sought by users is related to events. We showed that to meet the requirements of emerging systems, we have to synthesize and build on past experience, but not be limited by any specific discipline. The model E* captures attributes of events as well as different types of relationships among events.

It is important to store all events and their characteristics, but much information about events is captured in different types of relationships among them. Moreover, the granularity of an event such as a 'paper presentation event' or a 'conference event' must be considered carefully and techniques to relate them need to be defined and developed. One could derive attributes of an event from its sub-events at lower granularity or inherit attributes from its super-events. It is shown that many interesting relationships among places and other attributes could be discovered using the constraints defined for events and their instances. These aspects of event systems are novel and have not yet received much attention, but they are going to become increasingly crucial in implementing emerging systems. It is important to capture all requirements in a conceptual model and ascertain logical consistency for different operations that must be performed in the context of this model. To build an information system, one must consider implementation aspect of such a model in the context of a complete system. We devote the next chapter to the implementation consideration for model E* using data definition language that we call E*ML. We describe how we can adopt best practices from many databases, ranging from extended entity relationships to open data types recently introduced in Asterix system, and web systems and build on these to implement E*. Details of implementation are presented using the running example from political events. In addition to defining attributes of space, time, and entities, we presented in details approaches to define relationships among events and sub-events and to specify constraints among them. A function-based approach was used to detect and extract information from experiential data, such as video, to populate attributes of events and sub-events. For scalability and efficiency, storage structures for this hybrid model were considered and defined. A major goal of the Chapter 3 is to provide tools and techniques for implementing a system to deal with real world events.

Once we know how to implement and organize all information about events, we must also provide appropriate query language and query environment for users to interact with the system. Assuming that an event information system stores all information related to events, a query language should be developed to explore all aspects of queries, including their attributes and relationships among them. The first step in this is to characterize event queries. After considering different types of event queries, we discuss processing architecture for event query systems. This systems uses hybrid architecture that combines relational feature store for media, a file system as media store, and entity partitioned triple store. Such an approach is essential to build these emerging systems. Details of the processing approach and operators are discussed to show how event-query systems can be implemented.

So far in our discussion, we considered how events should be viewed, showed how to model different aspects of events using $E^*$ and showed how different types of queries could be articulated using such event information systems. Our approach builds on powerful concepts that emerged in information systems, and also in ontology and Web systems. To make all this discussion more grounded, we then discussed an emerging application area, Actionable Personal Intelligence, which uses events extensively. A human life could be considered a sequence of events. Approaches are being developed to capture all aspects of a person's life and store it for recollecting, reflecting, retrieving, recalling, and reminiscing about events and related information and experiences. This data must be organized using an event information system to provide an environment for people to make best use of the data for improving their life as well as for analyzing events and experiences and enjoying them. We discussed how this data will appear and presented example event queries for creating personal intelligence systems that will provide actionable information. We believe that many business applications, such as business intelligence, will also benefit significantly from similar approach.

As we all know, storytelling is one of the most important human activity. We all like to share stories. Most of the stories are closely related to events. Behind every story is a collection of events that the storyteller uses. To provide an interesting example of how event information systems will be used, we conclude with storytelling with events. An event information system could be considered a graph of all events, objects, their attributes, and relationships among them. A story is then a sub-graph that is selected by the storyteller based on the story he wants to tell a specific audience. A story request language builds on logical language and algebraic operators in the event language to specify what should go in the story. This allows selection of the sub-graph that could be used in the story. The storytelling process is considered a multistep process that selects appropriate events, ranks them based on different factors, and selects material, including the media associated, related to those events. Once all material for the relevant story has been selected, tools for storyteller to annotate the story with his/her additions and presentation environment to present a multimedia story should be provided. All these aspects are part of the discussion of storytelling.

Our goal in this book was to present emerging approaches for building event information systems that consider events as first class citizen and can be used to build emerging dynamic systems that are becoming common. In doing so, we reviewed existing approaches in many areas and presented a unified approach that adopts best practices from different applications to build next generation event systems. We believe that event information systems are the next frontier in information systems. To implement systems that seamlessly connect traditional information systems that mostly operated in the so called cyberspace to the real world using different types of sensors, such systems are essential. Concepts and techniques presented in this book will help in this.

# APPENDIX A

# An RDF Primer

Following [Gutierrez et al., 2004, Hayes, Ed.], the RDF graph data model is based on three infinite sets: $U$, the set of URI references, $B$, the set of "blank nodes," and $L$, the set of literals. A triple $(v_1, v_2, v_3) \in (U \cup B) \times U \times (U \cup B \cup L)$ is called an *RDF triple* where $v_1, v_2, v_3$ are called *subject*, *predicate* and *object*, respectively. An *RDF graph G* is a set of RDF triples. Figure A.1 shows an RDF graph.

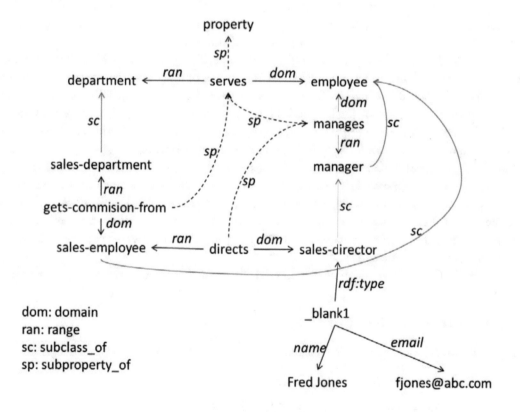

dom: domain
ran: range
sc: subclass_of
sp: subproperty_of

**Figure A.1:** An RDF Graph. In this figure, we have not used formal URIs for the node and edge labels. We have represented the edge of the graph in two ways − 1) by representing it as a special node whose domain and range are specified, and 2) as an edge label. These two styles of representation are used interchangeably in the book.

Every edge in the graph represents an RDF triple. The "blank node" in RDF has a special significance. It can be thought of as a graph node that stands for an abstract concept. In the figure, the blank node represents an instance of "sales director" whose name and email properties are specified. An RDF graph with no blank node is called *ground*.

Let $\mu$ be a mapping from a node set to a node set such that the URIs and literals are preserved in the mapping, but a blank node may be mapped to a URI or a literal. For an RDF graph $G$, $\mu(G)$ refers to the graph where a triple $(s, p, o) \in G$ is mapped to $(\mu(s), \mu(p), \mu(o))$. If such a $\mu(G)$ graph satisfies the condition that if $s$ is a subject in $G$, $\mu(s)$ is also a subject $G$, if $p$ is a predicate $G$, $\mu(p)$ is also a predicate in $G$, etc., then $\mu(G)$ is called an *instance* of $G$. Further, if $\mu(G)$ is such that the mapping produces fewer blank nodes, i.e., a blank node of $G$ maps to a URI or literal of $\mu(G)$ or two blank nodes of $G$ map to a single blank node of $\mu(G)$, then $\mu(G)$ is a called a *proper* instance of $G$. An RDF graph $G'$ is a *subgraph* of RDF graph $G$ if the set of triples of $G'$ is a subset of the set of triples of $G$. The *union* of $G_1$, $G_2$, denoted $G_1 \cup G_2$, is the set theoretical union of their sets of triples. The *merge* of $G_1$, $G_2$, denoted $G_1 + G_2$, is the union $G_1 \cup G_2'$, where $G_2'$ is an isomorphic copy of $G_2$ whose set of blank nodes is disjoint with that of $G_1$.

RDF Schema or RDF vocabulary [Gutierrez et al., 2004] defines the following. *Classes* are sets of resources. Elements of a class are known as instances of that class. To state that a resource is an instance of a class, the property rdf:type may be used (see Figure A.1. The following are the most important classes *rdfs:Resource* [res], *rdfs:Class* [class], *rdfs:Literal* [literal], *rdfs:Datatype* [datatype], *rdf:XMLLiteral* [xmlLit], and *rdf:Property* [prop]. Properties are binary relations between subject resources and object resources. The built-in properties are as follows: *rdfs:range* [range], *rdfs:domain* [dom], *rdf:type* [type], *rdfs:subClassOf* [sc], and *rdfs:subPropertyOf* [sp].

The reification vocabulary was designed to allow making statements about statements. It consists of *rdf:Statement* [stat], *rdf:subject* [subj], *rdf:predicate* [pred], and *rdf:object* [obj]. If (John loves Mary) is an RDF triple, we can reify it by creating an RDF statement R01 such that (R01 rdf:type rdf:statement),(R01 subject John), (R01 predicate loves), (R01 object Mary) are also valid triples.

Finally, the RDF vocabularies are endowed with a number of built-in rules. These are stated below.

**Existential Rule.** If $\mu : G \to G'$ is a mapping, then $G$ implies $G'$.

**Typing Rules.** These are type inference rules

    1. (a dom c), (a x y) implies (x type c)

    2. (a range d), (x a y) implies (y type d)

**Subclass Rules.** sc is reflexive and transitive

    1. (a type class) implies (a sc a)

    2. (a sc b), (b sc c) implies (a sc c)

3. (a sc b), (x type a) implies (x type b)

**Subproperty Rules.** sp is reflexive and transitive

1. (a type prop) implies (a sp a)

2. (a sp b), (b sp c) implies (a sp c)

3. (a sp b), (x a y) implies (x b y)

# Bibliography

Daniel J. Abadi, Samuel Madden, and Wolfgang Lindner. REED: robust, efficient filtering and event detection in sensor networks. In *Proc. of the 31st Int. Conf. on Very large data bases,* pages 769–780, 2005. Cited on page(s) 9

Daniel J. Abadi, Adam Marcus, Samuel Madden, and Katherine J. Hollenbach. Scalable semantic web data management using vertical partitioning. In *Proc. of the 33rd Int. Conf. on VLDB,* pages 411–422, 2007. Cited on page(s) 60, 61

Serge Abiteboul, Omar Benjelloun, and Tova Milo. The active xml project: an overview. 17(5): 1019–1040, 2008. DOI: 10.1007/s00778-007-0049-y Cited on page(s) 55

Raman Adaikkalavan and Sharma Chakravarthy. Snoopib: interval-based event specification and detection for active databases. *Data Knowl. Eng.,* 59:139–165, October 2006. DOI: 10.1016/j.datak.2005.07.009 Cited on page(s) 67

Asaf Adi and Opher Etzion. Amit - the situation manager. *The VLDB Journal,* 13(2):177–203, 2004. DOI: 10.1007/s00778-003-0108-y Cited on page(s) 6

Jagrati Agrawal, Yanlei Diao, Daniel Gyllstrom, and Neil Immerman. Efficient pattern matching over event streams. In *Proc. of the ACM Int. Conference on Management of Data,* pages 147–160, New York, NY, USA, 2008. ACM. DOI: 10.1145/1376616.1376634 Cited on page(s) 7, 9

Lina Al-Jadir, Christine Parent, and Stefano Spaccapietra. Reasoning with large ontologies stored in relational databases: The ontomind approach. *Data Knowl. Eng.,* 69(11):1158–1180, 2010. DOI: 10.1016/j.datak.2010.07.006 Cited on page(s) 58

Faisal Alkhateeb, Jean-François Baget, and Jérôme Euzenat. Extending sparql with regular expression patterns (for querying rdf). *Web Semant.,* 7:57–73, April 2009. DOI: 10.1016/j.websem.2009.02.002 Cited on page(s) 70

James F. Allen and George Ferguson. Actions and events in interval temporal logic. Technical report, Rochester, NY, USA, 1994. DOI: 10.1007/978-0-585-28322-7_7 Cited on page(s) 72

Alessandro Artale and Enrico Franconi. Foundations of temporal conceptual data models. In *Conceptual Modeling: Foundations and Applications: Essays in Honor of John Mylopoulos,* pages 10–35, 2009. DOI: 10.1007/978-3-642-02463-4_2 Cited on page(s) 17, 19

Alessandro Artale, Enrico Franconi, Nicola Guarino, and Luca Pazzi. Part-whole relations in object-centered systems: an overview. *Data and Knowl. Eng.*, 20(3):347–383, 1996. DOI: 10.1016/S0169-023X(96)00013-4 Cited on page(s) 33

Alessandro Artale, Carsten Lutz, and David Toman. A description logic of change. In *Proc. of the 20th Int. Joint Conf. on Artificial Intelligence*, pages 218–223, 2007. Cited on page(s) 17

Alessandro Artale, Roman Kontchakov, Vladislav Ryzhikov, and Michael Zakharyaschev. Complexity of reasoning over temporal data models. In *Proc. of the 29th Int. Conf. on Conceptual Modeling*, pages 174–187, 2010. DOI: 10.1007/978-3-642-16373-9_13 Cited on page(s) 37

Sotiris Batsakis and Euripides G. M. Petrakis. Sowl: spatio-temporal representation, reasoning and querying over the semantic web. In *Proc. of the 6th Int. Conf. on Semantic Systems*, pages 1–9, New York, NY, USA, 2010. ACM. DOI: 10.1145/1839707.1839726 Cited on page(s) 21

C. Beeri and R. Ramakrishnan. On the power of magic. In *Proc. of the 6th ACM Symp. on Principles of Database Syst.* , pages 269–284, 1987. DOI: 10.1145/28659.28689 Cited on page(s) 74

Alexander Behm, Vinayak R. Borkar, Michael J. Carey, Raman Grover, Chen Li, Nicola Onose, Rares Vernica, Alin Deutsch, Yannis Papakonstantinou, and Vassilis J. Tsotras. AS-TERIX: Towards a Scalable, Semistructured Data Platform for Evolving-World Models. *Distributed and Parallel Databases (special issue on Cloud Computing)*, page (to appear), 2011. DOI: 10.1007/s10619-011-7082-y Cited on page(s) 49

E. Bertino, E. Ferrari, and G. Guerrini. An approach to model and query event-based temporal data. In *Proc. of the 5th Int. Workshop on Temporal Representation and Reasoning*, pages 122–131, 1998. DOI: 10.1109/TIME.1998.674141 Cited on page(s) 16

Claudio Bettini, Curtis E. Dyreson, William S. Evans, Richard T. Snodgrass, and Xiaoyang Sean Wang. A glossary of time granularity concepts. In *Temporal Databases, Dagstuhl*, pages 406–413, 1997. DOI: 10.1007/BFb0053711 Cited on page(s) 30

Philip Bramsen, Pawan Deshpande, Yoong Keok Lee, and Regina Barzilay. Inducing temporal graphs. In *Proc. of the Conf. on Empirical Methods in Natural Language Processing*, pages 189–198, 2006. DOI: 10.3115/1610075.1610105 Cited on page(s) 85, 86

Lars Brenna, Alan Demers, Johannes Gehrke, Mingsheng Hong, Joel Ossher, Biswanath Panda, Mirek Riedewald, Mohit Thatte, and Walker White. Cayuga: a high-performance event processing engine. In *Proc. of the ACM Int. Conf. on Management of Data*, pages 1100–1102, New York, NY, USA, 2007. ACM. DOI: 10.1145/1247480.1247620 Cited on page(s) 7

Sergey Brin and Lawrence Page. The anatomy of a large-scale hypertextual web search engine. *Comput. Netw. ISDN Syst.*, 30(1-7):107–117, 1998. ISSN 0169-7552. DOI: 10.1016/S0169-7552(98)00110-X Cited on page(s) 81

Christoph Brochhaus, Jost Enderle, Achim Schlosser, Thomas Seidl, and Knut Stolze. Integrating the relational interval tree into ibm's db2 universal database server. In *Proc. of Daten. in Business, Tech. und Web, 11. Fachtagung des GI-Fachbereichs "Datenbanken und Informationssysteme"*, pages 67–86, 2005. Cited on page(s) 62

Kevin M. Brooks. Do story agents use rocking chairs? the theory and implementation of one model for computational narrative. In *Proc. of the 4th ACM Int. Conf. on Multimedia*, pages 317–328, 1996. DOI: 10.1145/244130.244233 Cited on page(s) 83

Nicolas Bruno, Luis Gravano, Nick Koudas, and Divesh Srivastava. Navigation- vs. index-based xml multi-query processing. In *Proc. of the 19th Int. Conf. on Data Engineering*, pages 139–150, 2003. DOI: 10.1109/ICDE.2003.1260788 Cited on page(s) 67

Alejandro Buchmann and Boris Koldehofe. Complex event processing. *it - Information Technology*, 51(5):241–242, 2009. DOI: 10.1524/itit.2009.9058 Cited on page(s) 6

Elena Camossi, Michela Bertolotto, and Elisa Bertino. A multigranular object-oriented framework supporting spatio-temporal granularity conversions. *Int. Journal of Geographical Information Science*, 20(5):511–534, 2006. DOI: 10.1080/13658810600607451 Cited on page(s) 31

Zhao Cao, Yanlei Diao, and Prashant Shenoy. Architectural considerations for distributed rfid tracking and monitoring. In *Proc. of the 5th Int. Workshop on Networking Meets Databases*, Oct. 2009. Cited on page(s) 9

M. Cavazza, R. Champagnat, and R. Leonardi. The IRIS Network of Excellence: Future Directions in Interactive Storytelling. *Interactive Storytelling*, pages 8–13, 2009. DOI: 10.1007/978-3-642-10643-9_4 Cited on page(s) 83

S. Chakravarty, V. Krishnaprasad, E. Anwar, and S.-K. Kim. Composite events for active database: Semantics, contexts, and detection. In *Proc. of 20th Int. Conf. on Very Large Data Bases, Santiago, Chile*, pages 609–617, Spetember 1994. Cited on page(s) 5, 6

Surajit Chaudhuri, Luis Gravano, and Amelie Marian. Optimizing top-k selection queries over multimedia repositories. *IEEE Trans. on Knowl. and Data Eng.*, 16:992–1009, August 2004. DOI: 10.1109/TKDE.2004.30 Cited on page(s) 64

Jun Chen and Jie Jiang. An event-based approach to spatio-temporal data modeling in land subdivision systems. *GeoInformatica*, 4:387–402, 2000. DOI: 10.1023/A:1026565929263 Cited on page(s) 7

Li Chen, Amarnath Gupta, and M. Erdem Kurul. Stack-based algorithms for pattern matching on DAGs. In *Proc. 31st Int. Conf. on Very Large Databases, Stockholm*, pages 493–504, 2005. Cited on page(s) 79

Zhimin Chen, H. V. Jagadish, Laks V. S. Lakshmanan, and Stelios Paparizos. From tree patterns to generalized tree patterns: On efficient evaluation of XQuery. In *Proc. of 29th Int. Conf. on Very Large Data Bases, Berlin, Germany*, pages 237–248, September 2003. Cited on page(s) 67

Rudi Cilibrasi and Paul M. B. Vitányi. The google similarity distance. *IEEE Trans. Knowl. Data Eng.*, 19(3):370–383, 2007. DOI: 10.1109/TKDE.2007.48 Cited on page(s) 93

Carlo Combi, Massimo Franceschet, and Adriano Peron. Representing and reasoning about temporal granularities. *J. of Logic and Computation*, 14(1):51–77, 2004. DOI: 10.1093/logcom/14.1.51 Cited on page(s) 30

Carlo Combi, Sara Degani, and Christian S. Jensen. Capturing temporal constraints in temporal er models. In *Proc. of the 27th Int. Conf. on Conceptual Modeling*, pages 397–411, 2008. DOI: 10.1007/978-3-540-87877-3_29 Cited on page(s) 17, 18, 40

T. Cormen, C. Leiserson, and R. Rivest. *Introduction to Algorithms*. The MIT Press, Cambridge, MA, 1990. Cited on page(s) 62

Umeshwar Dayal, Alejandro P. Buchmann, and Dennis R. McCarthy. Rules are objects too: A knowledge model for an active, object-oriented database system. In *2nd Int. Workshop on Object-Oriented Database Systems*, pages 129–143, Sept. 1988. DOI: 10.1007/3-540-50345-5_9 Cited on page(s) 5

W. Eisner. *Comics & sequential art*. North Light, 2005. Cited on page(s) 95

Ahmet Ekin, A. Murat Tekalp, and Rajiv Mehrotra. Automatic soccer video analysis and summarization. *IEEE Transactions on Image Processing*, 12(7):796–807, 2003. DOI: 10.1109/TIP.2003.812758 Cited on page(s) 10

Ramez Elmasri and Shamkant B. Navathe. *Fundamentals of Database Systems, 2nd Edition*. Benjamin/Cummings, 1994. Cited on page(s) 17, 39

Jost Enderle, Nicole Schneider, and Thomas Seidl. Efficiently processing queries on interval-and-value tuples in relational databases. In *Proc. 31st Int. Conf. on Very Large Data Bases*, pages 385–396, 2005. Cited on page(s) 62

Opher Etzion and Peter Niblett. *Event Processing in Action*. Manning Publications Company, 1 edition, August 2010. Cited on page(s) 7

A. Gangemi, N. Guarino, C. Masolo, A. Oltramari, and L. Schneider. Sweetening ontologies with DOLCE. In *Proc. 13th Int. Conf. on Knowl. Engineering and Knowl. Management Ontologies and the Semantic Web*, pages 166–181. Springer, 2002. DOI: 10.1007/3-540-45810-7_18 Cited on page(s) 12, 20, 21, 25

Hector Garcia-Molina, Jeffrey D. Ullman, and Jennifer Widom. *Database Systems – the Complete Book*. Pearson Hall, 2002. Cited on page(s) 67, 72

Stella Gatziu, Andreas Geppert, and Klaus R. Dittrich. Integrating active concepts into an object-oriented database system. In *Proc. of the 3rd Int. Workshop on Database Prog. Languages* , pages 399–415, San Francisco, CA, USA, 1992. Morgan Kaufmann Publishers Inc. Cited on page(s) 5

Narain H. Gehani and H. V. Jagadish. Active database facilities in ode. In *Active Database Systems: Triggers and Rules For Advanced Database Processing*, pages 207–232. Morgan Kaufmann, 1996. Cited on page(s) 5

Jim Gemmell, Gordon Bell, and Roger Lueder. MyLifeBits: a personal database for everything. *Commun. ACM*, 49(1):88–95, 2006. DOI: 10.1145/1107458.1107460 Cited on page(s) 1, 104

Risto Gligorov, Warner ten Kate, Zharko Aleksovski, and Frank van Harmelen. Using google distance to weight approximate ontology matches. In *Proc. of the 16th Int. Conf. on World Wide Web*, pages 767–776, 2007. DOI: 10.1145/1242572.1242676 Cited on page(s) 93

Bo Gong and Ramesh Jain. Segmenting photo streams in events based on optical metadata. In *Proc. of the 1st IEEE Int. Conf. on Semantic Computing*, pages 71–78, 2007. DOI: 10.1109/ICSC.2007.88 Cited on page(s) 55

Heidi Gregersen. The formal semantics of the timeer model. In *Proc. of the 3rd Asia Pacific Conf. on Conceptual Modeling*, pages 35–44, 2006. Cited on page(s) 40

Heidi Gregersen and Christian S. Jensen. Temporal entity-relationship models - a survey. *IEEE Trans. Knowl. Data Eng.*, 11(3):464–497, 1999. DOI: 10.1109/69.774104 Cited on page(s) 17

Amarnath Gupta and Simone Santini. Toward feature algebras in visual databases: The case for a histogram algebra. In *Proc. of the 5th Working Conference on Visual Database Systems*, pages 177–198, 2000. Cited on page(s) 64

Amarnath Gupta, Bin Liu, Pilho Kim, and Ramesh Jain. Using stream semantics for continuous queries in media stream processors. In *Int. Conf. on Data Engineering*, page 854, 2004. DOI: 10.1109/ICDE.2004.1320083 Cited on page(s) 1

Amarnath Gupta, Christopher Condit, and Xufei Qian. Biodb: An ontology-enhanced information system for heterogeneous biological information. *Data Knowl. Eng.*, 69(11):1084–1102, 2010. DOI: 10.1016/j.datak.2010.07.003 Cited on page(s) 76, 79

C. Gutierrez, C. Hurtado, and A. Mendelzon. Foundations of semantic web databases. In *ACM Symposium on Principles of Database Systems*, pages 95–106. ACM Press, June 2004. DOI: 10.1145/1055558.1055573 Cited on page(s) 111, 112

Claudio Gutierrez, Carlos A. Hurtado, and Alejandro Vaisman. Introducing time into RDF. *IEEE Trans. on Knowledge and Data Engineering*, 19(2):207–218, 2007. ISSN 1041-4347. DOI: 10.1109/TKDE.2007.34 Cited on page(s) 23

Gilberto A. Gutiérrez, Gonzalo Navarro, Andrea Rodríguez, Alejandro González, and José Orellana. A spatio-temporal access method based on snapshots and events. In *Proc. of the 13th ACM Int. workshop on Geographic information Systems*, pages 115–124, 2005. DOI: 10.1145/1097064.1097082 Cited on page(s) 8

Gilberto A. Gutiérrez, Gonzalo Navarro, and Andrea Rodríguez. Les-tree: A spatio-temporal access method based on snapshots and events. Technical Report TR-DCC-2008-014, Department of Computer Science, University of Chile, 2008. Cited on page(s) 8

A. Hampapur, L. Brown, J. Connell, A. Ekin, N. Haas, M. Lu, H. Merkl, and S. Pankanti. Smart video surveillance: exploring the concept of multiscale spatiotemporal tracking. *Signal Processing Magazine, IEEE*, 22(2):38 – 51, March 2005. DOI: 10.1109/MSP.2005.1406476 Cited on page(s) 55

Patrick Hayes(Ed.). Rdf semantics. W3C Proposal, Feb. 2004. http://www.w3.org/TR/rdf-mt/. Cited on page(s) 111

Huahai He and Ambuj K. Singh. Graphs-at-a-time: query language and access methods for graph databases. In *Proc. of the ACM Int. Conf. on Management of Data*, pages 405–418, 2008. DOI: 10.1145/1376616.1376660 Cited on page(s) 79

Joseph M. Hellerstein and Michael Stonebraker. Predicate migration: optimizing queries with expensive predicates. In *Proc. of the ACM Int. Conf. on Management of Data*, pages 267–276, 1993. DOI: 10.1145/170036.170078 Cited on page(s) 64

Stijn Heymans, Li Ma, Darko Anicic, Zhilei Ma, Nathalie Steinmetz, Yue Pan, Jing Mei, Achille Fokoue, Aditya Kalyanpur, Aaron Kershenbaum, Edith Schonberg, Kavitha Srinivas, Cristina Feier, Graham Hench, Branimir Wetzstein, and Uwe Keller. Ontology reasoning with large data repositories. In *Ontology Management*, Semantic Web And Beyond Computing for Human Experience, pages 89–128. Springer, 2008. DOI: 10.1007/978-0-387-69900-4_4 Cited on page(s) 46, 58

Jerry R. Hobbs and Feng Pan. An ontology of time for the semantic web. *ACM Trans. Asian Lang. Inf. Process.*, 3(1), 2004. DOI: 10.1145/1017068.1017073 Cited on page(s) 47

Dehainsala Hondjack, Guy Pierra, and Ladjel Bellatreche. Ontodb: An ontology-based database for data intensive applications. In *Database Systems for Advanced Applications*, pages 497–508, 2007. DOI: 10.1145/1017068.1017073 Cited on page(s) 58

Kathleen Stewart Hornsby and Stephen J. Cole. Modeling moving geospatial objects from an event-based perspective. *Transactions in GIS*, 11(4):555–573, 2007.
DOI: 10.1007/978-3-540-71703-4_43 Cited on page(s) 8

S. Idreos, M. L. Kersten, and S. Manegold. Self-Organizing Tuple Reconstruction In Column-Stores. In *Proc. of the Int. Conf. on Management of Data*, pages 297 – 308. ACM, June 2009.
DOI: 10.1145/1559845.1559878 Cited on page(s) 61

Ramesh Jain. Eventweb: Developing a human-centered computing system. *Computer*, 41:42–50, 2008. DOI: 10.1109/MC.2008.49 Cited on page(s) 104

Haifeng Jiang, Wei Wang, Hongjun Lu, and Jeffrey Xu Yu. Holistic twig joins on indexed XML documents. In *29th Conf. on Very Large Databases, Berlin, Germany*, pages 263–274. Morgan Kaufmann, September 2003. Cited on page(s) 67

Catharina Maria Keet. *A Formal Theory of Granularity*. PhD dissertation, Free University of Bozen Bolzano, Faculty of Computer Science, Apr. 2008. Cited on page(s) 29

Y. Kompatsiaris and P. Hobson. *Semantic Multimedia and Ontologies: Theory and Applications*. Springer-Verlag, 1st edition, Jan. 2008. Cited on page(s) 11

Vassilis Kostakos. Temporal graphs. *Physica A-statistical Mechanics and Its Applications*, 388:1007–1023, 2009. DOI: 10.1016/j.physa.2008.11.021 Cited on page(s) 85, 86

Carl Lagoze and Jane Hunter. The abc ontology and model. In *Proc. of the Int. Conf. on Dublin Core and Metadata Applications*, pages 160–176, 2001. Cited on page(s) 21

Sangkeun Lee, Gihyun Gong, Inbeom Hwang, and Sang-goo Lee. Lifelogon: A practical lifelog system for building and exploiting lifelog ontology. In *Proc/ of the IEEE Int. Conf. on Sensor Networks, Ubiquitous, and Trustworthy Computing*, pages 367–373, 2010. DOI: 10.1109/SUTC.2010.33 Cited on page(s) 104

Weiru Liu, Paul Miller, Jianbing Ma, and Weiqi Yan. Challenges of distributed intelligent surveillance system with heterogeneous information. In *Proc. of the workshop on Quantitative Risk Analysis for Security Applications*, pages 69–74, July 2009. Cited on page(s) 11

Nikos A. Lorentzos, Alexandra Poulovassilis, and Carol Small. Manipulation operations for an interval-extended relational model. *Data and Knowledge Engineering*, 17(1):1–29, 1995.
DOI: 10.1016/0169-023X(95)00022-K Cited on page(s) 14

David C. Luckham. *The Power of Events: An Introduction to Complex Event Processing in Distributed Enterprise Systems*. Addison-Wesley Longman Publishing Co., Inc., Boston, MA, USA, 2001. ISBN 0201727897. Cited on page(s) 6

Samuel R. Madden, Michael J. Franklin, Joseph M. Hellerstein, and Wei Hong. Tinydb: an acqui-sitional query processing system for sensor networks. *ACM Trans. Database Syst.*, 30(1):122–173, 2005. DOI: 10.1145/1061318.1061322 Cited on page(s) 8

Hooran MahmoudiNasab and Sherif Sakr. An experimental evaluation of relational rdf storage and querying techniques. In *Database Systems for Advanced Applications*, volume 6193 of *Lecture Notes in Computer Science*, pages 215–226. Springer Berlin / Heidelberg, 2010. DOI: 10.1007/978-3-642-14589-6_22 Cited on page(s) 60

Claudio Masolo, Stefano Borgo, Aldo Gangemi, Nicola Guarino, and Alessandro Oltramari. Won-derweb deliverable D18. Technical Report Del 18, Laboratory For Applied Ontology - ISTC-CNR, December 2003. Cited on page(s) 21

S. McCloud. *Understanding comics*. Kepustakaan Populer Gramedia, 1993. Cited on page(s) 95, 98

J. McGlothlin and L. Khan. RDFJoin: A Scalable Data Model for Persistence and Efficient Querying of RDF Datasets. Tech. Report UTDCS-08-09, Univ. of Texas at Dallas, 2008. Cited on page(s) 61, 75, 80

Isabella Merlo, Giovanna Guerrini, Elisa Bertino, Elena Ferrari, and Shashi Gadia. Querying multiple temporal granularity data. In *Proc. of the 7th Int. Workshop on Temporal Representation and Reasoning*, page 103, 2000. DOI: 10.1109/TIME.2000.856591 Cited on page(s) 30

Saket Navlakha, Rajeev Rastogi, and Nisheeth Shrivastava. Graph summarization with bounded error. In *Proc. of the 28th Int. Conf. on Management of Data*, pages 419–432, 2008. DOI: 10.1145/1376616.1376661 Cited on page(s) 99

Hannes Obweger, Martin Suntinger, Josef Schiefer, and Günther R. Raidl. Similarity searching in sequences of complex events. In *Proc. of the 4th IEEE Int. Conf. on Research Challenges in Information Science*, pages 631–640, 2010. DOI: 10.1109/RCIS.2010.5507284 Cited on page(s) 81

Norman W. Paton and Oscar Díaz. Active database systems. *ACM Comput. Surv.*, 31(1):63–103, 1999. DOI: 10.1145/311531.311623 Cited on page(s) 5

Jorge Pérez, Marcelo Arenas, and Claudio Gutierrez. nSPARQL: A navigational language for RDF. In *ISWC '08: Proc. of the 7th Int. Conf. on The Semantic Web*, pages 66–81, 2008. ISBN 978-3-540-88563-4. DOI: 10.1007/978-3-540-88564-1_5 Cited on page(s) 70

Matthew Perry. *A Framework To Support Spatial, Temporal and Thematic Analytics over Semantic Web Data*. PhD thesis, Wright State University, Dayton, Ohio, July 2008. Cited on page(s) 19, 21, 23, 26, 27, 46

Donna Peuquet and Niu Duan. An event-based spatiotemporal data model for temporal analysis of geographical data. *International Journal of Geographical Information Systems*, 9(1):7–24, 1995. DOI: 10.1080/02693799508902022 Cited on page(s) 7

Stefan Pfennigschmidt and Agns Voisard. Handling Temporal Granularity in Situation-Based Services. Technical Report TR-09-005, Fraunhofer Institute for Software and Systems Engineering, 2009. Cited on page(s) 30

Venkatesh Raghavan, Elke A. Rundensteiner, John Woycheese, and Abhishek Mukherji. Firestream: Sensor stream processing for monitoring fire spread. In *Proc. of the 23rd Int. Conf. on Data Engineering*, pages 1507–1508, 2007. DOI: 10.1109/ICDE.2007.369056 Cited on page(s) 9

Mark O. Riedl and Andrew Stern. Believable agents and intelligent story adaptation for interactive storytelling. In *Proc. of the 3rd Int. Conf. on Technologies for Interactive Digital Storytelling and Entertainment*, pages 1–12. Springer, 2006. DOI: 10.1007/11944577_1 Cited on page(s) 83

Shariq Rizvi. Complex event processing beyond active databases: Streams and uncertainties. Master's thesis, EECS Department, University of California, Berkeley, Dec 2005. Cited on page(s) 6

Royi Ronen and Oded Shmueli. Soql: A language for querying and creating data in social networks. In *Proc. of the IEEE Int. Conf. on Data Engineering*, pages 1595–1602, 2009. DOI: 10.1109/ICDE.2009.172 Cited on page(s) 67

Mukesh Kumar Saini, Mohan S. Kankanhalli, and Ramesh Jain. A flexible surveillance system architecture. In *Proc. of the 6th IEEE Int. Conf. on Advanced Video and Signal Based Surveillance*, pages 571–576, 2009. DOI: 10.1109/AVSS.2009.50 Cited on page(s) 11

Alberto Salguero, Cecilia Delgado, and Francisco Araque. STOWL: An owl extension for facilitating the definition of taxonomies in spatio-temporal ontologies. In *Visioning and Engineering the Knowledge Society. A Web Science Perspective*, volume 5736 of *Lecture Notes in Computer Science*, pages 336–345. Springer, 2009. DOI: 10.1007/978-3-642-04754-1_35 Cited on page(s) 21

Arjun Satish, Ramesh Jain, and Amarnath Gupta. Tolkien: An event based storytelling system. *PVLDB*, 2(2):1630–1633, Aug. 2009. Cited on page(s) 94

Arjun Satish, Ramesh Jain, and Amarnath Gupta. Tolkien: Weaving Stories from Personal Media. Technical Report ESL.UCI.EDU-TR 2010/04/11, Univ. of California Irvine, 2010. Cited on page(s) 95, 96

Ansgar Scherp, Thomas Franz, Carsten Saathoff, and Steffen Staab. F–a model of events based on the foundational ontology dolce+dns ultralight. In *Proc. of the 5th Int. Conf. on Knowledge Capture*, pages 137–144, 2009a. DOI: 10.1145/1597735.1597760 Cited on page(s) 19, 43

Ansgar Scherp, Symeon Papadopoulos, and et al. Apostolos Kritikos. Workpackage d5.2.1: Prototypical knowledge management methodology. Final Report FP7-215453, WeKnowIt Consortium, 2009b. Cited on page(s) 46

Lefteris Sidirourgos, Romulo Goncalves, Martin L. Kersten, Niels Nes, and Stefan Manegold. Column-store support for rdf data management: not all swans are white. *PVLDB*, 1(2):1553–1563, 2008. Cited on page(s) 60, 61

Vivek K. Singh, Mingyan Gao, and Ramesh Jain. Social pixels: genesis and evaluation. In *Proc. of the ACM Int. Conf. on Multimedia*, pages 481–490, 2010. DOI: 10.1145/1873951.1874030 Cited on page(s) 77

Richard T. Snodgrass and Ilsoo Ahn. Temporal databases. *IEEE Computer*, 19(9):35–42, Sept. 1986. DOI: 10.1109/MC.1986.1663327 Cited on page(s) 14

Stefano Spaccapietra, Christine Parent, and Esteban Zimanyi. Modeling time from a conceptual perspective. In *Proc. of the 7th Int. Conf. on Information and Knowledge Management*, pages 432–440, 1998. DOI: 10.1145/288627.288693 Cited on page(s) 18

Michael Stonebraker, Daniel J. Abadi, Adam Batkin, Xuedong Chen, Mitch Cherniack, Miguel Ferreira, Edmond Lau, Amerson Lin, Samuel Madden, Elizabeth J. O'Neil, Patrick E. O'Neil, Alex Rasin, Nga Tran, and Stanley B. Zdonik. C-store: A column-oriented dbms. In *Proc. of Int. Conf. on Very Large Databases*, pages 553–564. ACM, 2005. Cited on page(s) 60

Martin Suntinger. Event-based similarity search and its applications in business analytics. Master's thesis, Fakultät für Informatik der Technischen Universität Wien, 2009. Cited on page(s) 81

Carolyn L. Talcott. Cyber-physical systems and events. In *Software-Intensive Systems and New Computing Paradigms*, pages 101–115. Springer, 2008. DOI: 10.1007/978-3-540-89437-7_6 Cited on page(s) 8

Abdullah Uz Tansel. Temporal relational data model. *IEEE Trans. Knowl. Data Eng.*, 9(3):464–479, 1997. DOI: 10.1109/69.599934 Cited on page(s) 15

Paolo Terenziani, Richard T. Snodgrass, Alessio Bottrighi, Mauro Torchio, and Gianpaolo Molino. Extending temporal databases to deal with telic/atelic medical data. *Artif. Intell. Med.*, 39:113–126, February 2007. DOI: 10.1016/j.artmed.2006.08.003 Cited on page(s) 13

Kia Teymourian and Adrian Paschke. Towards semantic event processing. In *Proc. of the 3rd ACM Int. Conf. on Distributed Event-Based Systems*, pages 1–2, 2009. DOI: 10.1145/1619258.1619296 Cited on page(s) 7

Yannis Theoharis, Vassilis Christophides, and Gregory Karvounarakis. Benchmarking database representations of rdf/s stores. In *Proc. of the 4th Int. Semantic Web Conference*, pages 685–701, 2005. DOI: 10.1007/11574620_49 Cited on page(s) 58

Ying-li Tian, Lisa Brown, Arun Hampapur, Max Lu, Andrew Senior, and Chiao-fe Shu. IBM smart surveillance system (S3): event based video surveillance system with an open and extensible framework. *Mach. Vision Appl.*, 19(5-6):315–327, 2008a. DOI: 10.1007/s00138-008-0153-z Cited on page(s) 1, 10

Yuanyuan Tian, Richard A. Hankins, and Jignesh M. Patel. Efficient aggregation for graph summarization. In *Proc. of the 28th Int. Conf. on Management of Data*, pages 567–580, 2008b. DOI: 10.1145/1376616.1376675 Cited on page(s) 99

Hanghang Tong and Christos Faloutsos. Center-piece subgraphs: problem definition and fast solutions. In *Proc. of the 12th ACM Int. Conf. on Knowledge Discovery and Data Mining*, pages 404–413, 2006. DOI: 10.1145/1150402.1150448 Cited on page(s) 79

Octavian Udrea, Diego Reforgiato Recupero, and V. S. Subrahmanian. Annotated RDF. *ACM Trans. Comput. Logic*, 11(2):1–41, 2010. DOI: 10.1145/1656242.1656245 Cited on page(s) 23, 32, 33, 48

Willem Robert van Hage, V?ronique Malais?, Roxane Segers, Laura Hollink, and Guus Schreiber. Design and use of the simple event model (sem). *Web Semantics: Science, Services and Agents on the World Wide Web*, In Press, Corrected Proof:–, 2011. DOI: 10.1016/j.websem.2011.03.003 Cited on page(s) 19

Achille C. Varzi. Parts, wholes, and part-whole relations: the prospects of mereotopology. *Data Knowl. Eng.*, 20(3):259–286, 1996. DOI: 10.1016/S0169-023X(96)00017-1 Cited on page(s) 33

Agnes Voisard and Holger Ziekow. ARCHITECT: a layered framework for classifying technologies for event-based systems. *Information Systems*, 2011. DOI: 10.1016/j.is.2011.03.006 Cited on page(s) 1

Wenjun Wang, Wei Guo, Yingwei Luo, Xiaolin Wang, and Zhuoqun Xu. The study and application of crime emergency ontology event model. In *Proc. of the 9th Int. Conf. on Knowledge-Based Intelligent Information and Engineering Systems* (4), pages 806–812, 2005a. DOI: 10.1007/11554028_113 Cited on page(s) 21, 29

Wenjun Wang, Yingwei Luo, Xinpeng Liu, Xiaolin Wang, and Zhuoqun Xu. Ontological model of event for integration of inter-organization applications. In *Int. Conf. on Computational Science and Its Applications* , pages 301–310, 2005b. DOI: 10.1007/11424758_32 Cited on page(s) 21

Cathrin Weiss, Panagiotis Karras, and Abraham Bernstein. Hexastore: sextuple indexing for semantic web data management. *PVLDB*, 1(1):1008–1019, 2008. DOI: 10.1145/1453856.1453965 Cited on page(s) 61

Evan Welbourne, Nodira Khoussainova, Julie Letchner, Yang Li, Magdalena Balazinska, Gaetano Borriello, and Dan Suciu. Cascadia: A system for specifying, detecting, and managing RFID events. In *Proc. of the 6th Int. Conf. on Mobile systems, applications, and services*, pages 281–294, 2008. DOI: 10.1145/1378600.1378631 Cited on page(s) 1

Utz Westermann and Ramesh Jain. Toward a common event model for multimedia applications. *IEEE MultiMedia*, 14(1):19–29, 2007. ISSN 1070-986X. DOI: 10.1109/MMUL.2007.23 Cited on page(s) 21, 22, 43

Michael F. Worboys and Kathleen Hornsby. From objects to events: Gem, the geospatial event model. In *Proc. of the 3rd Int. Conf. on Geographic Information Science*, pages 327–344, 2004. DOI: 10.1007/978-3-540-30231-5_22 Cited on page(s) 7

Kengsheng Wu, K. Stockinger, and Arie Shoshani. Analysis of multi-level and multi-component compressed bitmap indexes. *ACM Trans. on Database Syst.*, 35(1):Article 2, Feb. 2010. DOI: 10.1145/1670243.1670245 Cited on page(s) 62

Lexing Xie and Rong Yan. Extracting semantics from multimedia content: Challenges and solutions. In A. Divakaran, editor, *Multimedia Content Analysis: Theory and Applications*. Springer-Verlag, 2008. Cited on page(s) 12

Lexing Xie, H. Sundaram, and M. Campbell. Event mining in multimedia streams. *Proceedings of the IEEE*, 96(4):623 –647, Apr. 2008. DOI: 10.1109/JPROC.2008.916362 Cited on page(s) 9, 10

Ziyou Xiong, R. Radhakrishnan, A. Divakaran, and T. S. Huang. Audio events detection based highlights extraction from baseball, golf and soccer games in a unified framework. In *Proc. of the Int. Conf. on Multimedia and Expo*, pages 401–404, 2003. DOI: 10.1109/ICASSP.2003.1200049 Cited on page(s) 10

Jeffrey Xu Yu and Jiefeng Cheng. Graph reachability queries: A survey. In Charu C. Aggarwal and Haixun Wang, editors, *Managing and Mining Graph Data*, volume 40 of *Advances in Database Systems*, pages 181–215. Springer US, 2010. Cited on page(s) 63

Ning Zhang, Yuanyuan Tian, and Jignesh M. Patel. Discovery-driven graph summarization. In *Proc. of the 26th Int. Conf. on Data Engineering*, pages 880–891, 2010. DOI: 10.1109/ICASSP.2003.1200049 Cited on page(s) 99

Peixiang Zhao and Jiawei Han. On graph query optimization in large networks. *Proc. VLDB Endow.*, 3:340–351, September 2010. Cited on page(s) 65

Detlef Zimmer and Rainer Unland. On the semantics of complex events in active database management systems. In *Proc. of the 15th Int. Conf. on Data Engineering*, page 392. IEEE Computer Society, 1999. DOI: 10.1109/ICDE.1999.754955 Cited on page(s) 6

# Authors' Biographies

## AMARNATH GUPTA

**Amarnath Gupta** is a Research Scientist at the San Diego Supercomputer Center of University of California San Diego. His current research interests are in the area of emerging information systems that include graph data management, semantic information integration for scientific applications, ontological information management, information management in social networks, and the impact of high-performance computing platforms for information systems problems. Before UCSD, he was at Virage, a multimedia information system company, and at the Indian Statistical Institute, Kolkata, India. He is a member of the ACM.

## RAMESH JAIN

**Ramesh Jain** is an entrepreneur, researcher, and educator. He is a Donald Bren Professor in Information & Computer Sciences at University of California, Irvine where he is doing research in Event Web and experiential computing. Earlier, he served on faculty of Georgia Tech, University of California at San Diego, The University of Michigan, Ann Arbor, Wayne State University, and Indian Institute of Technology, Kharagpur. He is a Fellow of ACM, IEEE, AAAI, IAPR, and SPIE. His current research interests are in searching multimedia data and creating EventWebs for experiential computing. He is the recipient of several awards including the ACM SIGMM Technical Achievement Award 2010. Ramesh co-founded several companies and has been advisor to several other companies including some of the largest companies in media and search space.

Printed in the United States
by Baker & Taylor Publisher Services